The Popular
Cocker Spaniel

by
H. S. Lloyd

Read Country Books
Home Farm
44 Evesham Road
Cookhill, Alcester
Warwickshire
B49 5lJ

www.readcountrybooks.com

ISBN No. 978-1-4067-9563-9

British Library Cataloguing-in-publication Data
A catalogue record for this book is available
from the British Library.

Read Country Books
Home Farm
44 Evesham Road
Cookhill, Alcester
Warwickshire
B49 5lJ

www.readcountrybooks.com

THE POPULAR
COCKER SPANIEL

ITS HISTORY, STRAINS, PEDIGREES, BREEDING, KENNEL
MANAGEMENT, AILMENTS, EXHIBITION, SHOW POINTS,
AND ELEMENTARY TRAINING FOR SPORT AND FIELD
TRIALS, WITH A LIST OF WINNING DOGS

BY

H. S. LLOYD
"OF WARE"

WITH AN INTRODUCTION TO
THE FOURTH EDITION BY
J. M. PORTER

Illustrated by HAY HUTCHISON

POPULAR DOGS PUBLISHING COMPANY LIMITED,
Australia House, Strand, London, W.C.2.

*Made and Printed in England by Watmoughs Limited,
and Published by Popular Dogs Publishing Company
Limited, Australia House, Strand, London, W.C.*

FIRST EDITION -   -   -   1924
SECOND EDITION   -   -   1929
THIRD EDITION -   •   -   1933
FOURTH EDITION   •   -   **1939**

CONTENTS

CHAPTER I

ORIGIN AND EARLY HISTORY.—Theories—Egyptian Monuments —Antiquity of the Spaniel—The Spaniel in English Literature—Dr. Caius and Spaniels—Sussex Spaniels— Charles I and his Spaniels—Retrieving Spaniels—Ancestry —Mr. C. A. Phillips on Field Spaniels and Cockers— "Stonehenge" on Welsh and Devonshire Cockers   1

CHAPTER II

DIVIDING LINE BETWEEN COCKERS AND FIELD SPANIELS.—A New Era—The Obos—The Kennel Club and Cockers— American Cockers and the Obos—The Brutons—The Rivingtons—Of Wares—Braesides—Bowdlers—Trumping-tons—The Doonys—The Galtrees—The Rocklyns—The Fulmers—The Pinbrooks—The Fairholmes—The Falcon-ers. *The Post-War Period:* Dominant Sires—The Bazels and Dunfords—The Blaedowns—The Byfleets—The Churchdenes—The Cobnars—The Conchietons—The Dob-rows—The Felbriggs—Of Fews—The Foxhams—The Glen-bervies—The Gulvals—The Hubbastones—The Melforts— The Ottershaws—The Oxshotts—Of Sauls—The Treetops —The Vivary—Cocker Spaniel Prefixes and Affixes   ...   15

CHAPTER III

PITFALLS FOR THE NOVICE.—Size of the Desired Kennel—The Brood Bitch as a Start—Purchasing a Puppy—The Glamour of a Prize Winner—Delusive Advertisements— Essentials for Breeding—Points to Avoid—Situation of the Kennel—Sleeping Accommodation—Design in Kennels —Cleanliness—Construction of Kennels—Sleeping Benches —Roofing—Shelter from Wind—Kennel Management— Worming the Brood Bitch—Worm Remedies—Disinfect-ants—Grooming—Beds—Meat Rations Essential—Times of Feeding—Vegetables—Puppy Rearing—Variation of Diet—Weaning—Artificial Heat—Treating Puppies for Worms—Puppies out at walk—Preparing for Exhibition— Teaching Ringcraft—Muscular Development—The Coat and its Care—Trimming—Washing—Etiquette of the Show Ring—Don'ts for Exhibitors   91

CHAPTER IV

FUNDAMENTAL PRINCIPLES OF BREEDING LIVE STOCK.—
Characteristics of Strain—Experiments—Mating Champion
Dog and Champion Bitch—Transmitting Faults—Sound-
ness—Tail Placement—Size in the Brood Bitch—"Type"
—Fashion in Cockers—In-breeding—Line Breeding—Best
Age for Stud Dog to sire Puppies—Undermining the
Constitution—Breeding Table—Rosslyn Bruce on Stud
Force—The Bitch's First Season—The Stud Dog—
Conditions for Service—Colour Breeding—Self-coloured
and Parti-coloured—Difficulty of Perpetuating Reds—
The Descriptive Standard of the Cocker Spaniel as adopted
by the Cocker Spaniel Club—The Scale of Points for
Judging Cocker Spaniels—The English Cocker in America 119

CHAPTER V

FIELD TRIALS FOR SPANIELS.—The Woodcock Spaniel—
Improvement of Working Qualities—Championship Stake
for Cockers—Game Finding—Retrieving—First Principles
of Training—Selecting a Puppy for Training—Working
to Signals—Ranging—Training with a "dummy"—
Working Upwind—Hunting and Questing—Flushing the
Game—"Foot" Scent and "Blood" Scent—Gun Shyness—
Training on Live Rabbits—The Check Cord—Dropping to
Fur—Dropping to Shot—Don'ts for Trainers—List of
Kennel Club Challenge Certificate Winners from 1910 to
1939 inclusive—List of Champion Cocker Spaniels (post-
war period)—Field Trial Champion Cocker Spaniels   ... 153

CHALLENGE CERTIFICATE WINNERS 1910-38   171

TITLE OF CHAMPION—How obtained   191

AN IMPORTANT 1932 KENNEL CLUB ANNOUNCEMENT 191

APPENDIX

COMMON DISEASES OF THE DOG.—Diseases of Puppyhood—
Diseases of Grown Dogs—Eye Troubles—Skin Troubles—
Mouth Troubles—Contagious and infectious fevers—Res-
piratory troubles—Digestive troubles—Diseases of the
Mother—Miscellaneous   195

INTRODUCTION TO FOURTH EDITION

By J. M. PORTER.

THE invitation from the Author of THE POPULAR COCKER SPANIEL to write an introduction to the Fourth Edition of his excellent book is such an unusual honour that I am almost " pen-shy."

I find I have still in my possession many letters from his father, the late Mr. R. Lloyd, going back as far as 1892, and from that correspondence I learnt much, and the source of interest possessed by the indefatigable Secretary of the Cocker Spaniel Club, as breeder of the highest class of Cockers, and an Author of all that appertains thereto, is easily inferred.

I note that in January, 1896, Mr. Lloyd, senior, mentions the fact that a then leading breeder was " coming round " to the short, cobby bodies, and quick and active action. The growing tendency towards this culminated early in the present century in a few conspirators venturing on the launching of the Cocker Spaniel Club, the gradual elimination of the long. low type, resulting in the great popularity of the breed, which so frequently to-day heads the list of entries at the great shows. For this the hard and continuous work of the Secretary, Mr. H. S. Lloyd, has been in great measure the vital force—long may he continue the good work.

J. M. PORTER.

" Braeside,"
    Colwyn Bay.
May, 1939.

INTRODUCTION TO THIRD EDITION
By E. C. SPENCER.

IT gives me pleasure to write a short introduction to the Third Edition of Mr. H. S. Lloyd's book, THE POPULAR COCKER SPANIEL. I am confident that there is no one who has had greater experience in breeding, showing, and field trials, or is better qualified to write on this most popular and grand little sporting dog. I remember Mr. Lloyd in his boyhood days assisting his late most respected father, Mr. Richard Lloyd, with his Cockers at shows, and the great help his father was in improving the breed in the early days. In passing I may mention many of us benefited through his assistance (he was the means of me breeding at least two champions). Like father like son, he is carrying on, and we owe to-day the great popularity of the Cocker Spaniel to Mr. H. S. Lloyd, and the great work he has done as Secretary of the Cocker Spaniel Club.

It is naturally most gratifying to me as one of the founders of the Club in 1902 that it is so efficiently carried on and has brought the breed to such a high pinnacle of fame.

As one of the oldest breeders, I am sure both the expert and novice will get interesting reading and knowledge in the perusal of this book.

E. C. SPENCER.

The Park,
    Overstone, Northants.   "Doony" Prefix.

INTRODUCTION TO SECOND EDITION

By Mrs. HESTER HIGGENS.

IT is a great pleasure to me to write these words of introduction to the Second Edition of THE POPULAR COCKER SPANIEL, for the Author is a very old and a very good friend of mine and I have to thank him for many kind and helpful words and actions.

Until the publication of the First Edition of this book there existed, in this country, no book dealing solely with the breed—rather a curious fact considering the numbers of people who were breeding Cockers and clamouring for a book of instruction—I can only conclude that there was nobody in existence who knew enough about Cockers to fill a book except Mr. Lloyd, and it was a great achievement on the part of the publishers of THE POPULAR COCKER SPANIEL to persuade him at last to put pen to paper.

There is no one whose opinion is of greater value to the novice and the " old hand " alike, than Mr. Lloyd, he knows his subject from A to Z, and he gives sound and practical advice on every page. It is, I think, a moot point if the man who breeds his winners or the man who buys them " in the rough " is the better judge of stock, but the word of the man who can do both certainly carries great weight. In my novice days Mr. Lloyd's opinion and advice were freely and generously given to me when asked for, and though my novice days are long past I still, when in doubt, apply to him for help.

The past history of the breed is of absorbing interest to those who take pedigrees seriously, as they ought to be taken, and it is interesting and helpful to know from which strains the leading modern kennels are descended. To those who crave success in the show ring I commend the instructions on preparation.

The amazing popularity of the Cocker has not diminished, and I am quite sure there is a steady progress in type and record. Just after the War when there were a number of new breeders and exhibitors who knew little of their subject, there was a craze in some quarters for a very long and narrow head, which was usually devoid of stops and, for some unknown reason, was often accompanied by flat ribs. Greater knowledge brought realization that these points, besides being antagonistic to true Cocker type, were unpractical and undesirable in other ways, and this " exaggerated type " is little accounted of in these days, but a certain amount of harm had been done, but during the last two years I am pleased to see a great improvement in ribs and quarters, and I am sure that the Cocker is better now than ever before. For this improvement some credit must be given to Mr. Lloyd, who has always been an eloquent advocate of the genuine Cocker.

HESTER HIGGENS.

The " Falconer " Cockers,
    Tarrant Monkton,
        Blandford.

September, 1929.

INTRODUCTION TO FIRST EDITION

By C. A. PHILLIPS.

IT is with the greatest pleasure I accede to Mr. Lloyd's request to write a short introduction for his book on the Cocker Spaniel. I do this not only on account of our long and pleasant friendship, but also for the great appreciation I have ever entertained for the memory of his father, the late Mr. Richard Lloyd, of Ware, one who did so much for the advancement of the Cocker in the early days of shows. Many years ago when I was endeavouring to establish the coloured variety in my own kennel, his sound advice helped me to overcome many difficulties. No one was so diffident when giving an opinion as he, but no opinion was of greater value when obtained. Ever a modest and generous rival when victorious, and always a true sportsman when defeated.

No excuse is necessary for writing an up-to-date monograph of the Cocker Spaniel in these days, for is it not, at the present time, the most popular of our breeds? I have, moreover, no hesitation in saying that this task could not be in more capable hands than those of the present Secretary of the Cocker Spaniel Club, for there is no one who has taken a more lively and helpful interest in the breed. His many past and present successes on the show bench and at field trials are a sufficient testimony to his great knowledge and insight of what is required at the present time.

None but those who have had experience are aware of the difficulties that have to be contended with in producing a book of this description. It entails a great amount of arduous labour and research, in order to discover any authentic record relating to the parent stock from which a breed is derived; for our earlier historians have left but a paucity of specific information on which to build any foundation, and even then some of these ancient authorities are misleading and contradictory.

It therefore becomes very obvious that Mr. Lloyd, by writing this book on the Cocker Spaniel, is not only supplying a very present need, but also a textbook of reference for those generations who shall succeed us.

There is certainly no intention on my part to travel the ground which has been so ably covered by the Author, and I feel somewhat diffident of dipping in my own oar. Nevertheless, I would like to remind those breeders who may have the privilege of reading this book of this fact, that, first and foremost, the Cocker Spaniel has been handed down to us by our ancestors as one of our best working gun-dogs, and, therefore, any improvement that may be added to his general appearance must in every way coincide with his utility as a workman.

There is no doubt the Cocker has changed more quickly in appearance and requirements than any other of the Spaniel family, but this is chiefly by reason of the changed methods of shooting. For this reason he has developed from the smaller unit of a team to the larger-sized " dog of all work," thereby adding to his popularity—but we cannot have it both ways. If he is to fulfil the requirements of to-day as a working dog, he must be of such a build, and such a size, to meet these altered conditions.

All breeders of experience recognise the fact that it is much more easy to breed quality in the diminutive specimen than in the larger-sized one, and were he required only for the show bench the question of size would not be of the same importance in the Cocker Spaniel.

Those who are personally acquainted with Mr. Lloyd know that the production of this book has been with him a labour of love, therefore it carries with it all the good wishes of his friends for its success.

C. A. PHILLIPS.

The " Rivington " Spaniels,
         Castle Douglas, N.B.
June, 1924.

Mr. H. S. Lloyd (the Author)
with the Blue Roan Cocker Spaniels Champion Invader of Ware,
Luckystar of Ware, champion of champions and Whoopee of Ware.

PREFACE

" Of all the dogs that are so sweet,
    The Spaniel is the most complete;
    Of all the Spaniels, dearest far
    The little loving Cockers are."

The More I See of Men—E. V. Lucas.

No more fitting opening to a book dealing with Cockers could be found than the foregoing, which was written by a true lover of this big-hearted little dog.

This monograph on the breed has been written at the request of many friends who have urged me to endeavour to place before the novice and newcomer to the breed a simply-written book dealing with the subject from a practical standpoint.

I make no claims to any literary genius, but the information contained herein has been gathered through a lifetime's experience of the dog I love. It is my sincere hope that this volume may prove of some assistance, and if it gives as much pleasure to the reader as it did to me in its compilation I am amply rewarded.

My warmest thanks are conferred on all those who have so kindly assisted me, both in collecting material, verifying statements, and the loan of photographs for reproduction.

H. S. Lloyd.

Swakeley's Farm,
    Ickenham,
        Middlesex.

CHAPTER I

Diminutive hunter, you're splendidly game,
With a very big heart in a very small frame;
You're a merry companion, a staunch little friend,
You will follow a line, or a pal, to the end.

A. R. H. Brown.

ORIGIN AND EARLY HISTORY

ORIGIN and Early History—Theories—Egyptian Monuments—Antiquity of the Spaniel—The Spaniel in English Literature—Dr. Caius and Spaniels—Sussex Spaniels—Charles I and His Spaniels—Retrieving Spaniels—Ancestry—Mr. C. A. Phillips on Field Spaniels and Cockers—"Stonehenge" on Welsh and Devonshire Cockers.

THEORIES as to the origin of the dog have been as numerous as they are unsatisfying. It is surmised that all our breeds are derived from an original stock and there is ample evidence to prove the existence of a semi-domesticated dog in prehistoric time. Further evidence of the taming of the wild species, *Canidæ*, is to be found in the remains left by the ancient cave-dwellers in the fossilised deposits discovered in Northern Europe, which attest the companionship of the dog to the earliest human beings of whom history makes mention.

Turning from a somewhat speculative aspect to that of actual records, Egyptian monuments of the Fourth Dynasty (B.C. 3500) depict hunting scenes wherein small quadrupeds with readily recognisable canine characteristics are to be found. In one such example from the tomb of Amtem, dogs of a greyhound conformation are portrayed in the pursuit of deer, and Assyrian bas-reliefs in the

B
1

British Museum show a dog, not unlike the present-day Mastiff, to have been as completely a companion of man and a helper in the chase as in our own times.

The antiquity of the Spaniel is undoubted.

In the Cypriote collection at the Metropolitan Museum, New York, is a small model which has all the appearance of a Spaniel (Plate I). Though the feet and tail are missing, the head, the coat, and the characteristic expression bear a distinct resemblance to a dog of this breed.

In English literature the first mention of the Spaniel is to be found in the *Wif of Bathe's Prologue*, by Chaucer (1340-1400), in which the famous author of the Canterbury Tales employed the simile, " For as a Spaynel she wol on him lepe," proving incontestably that the breed was familiarly known in England six centuries ago. Chaucer's contemporary, Gaston de Foix, who died in 1391, also alludes to the Spaniel in his *Miroir de Phœbus*. Another early mention of the Spaniel is in *The Master of Game*, by Edward Plantagenet, second Duke of York, who was killed at the Battle of Agincourt in 1415. This Duke of York was Master of Game to his uncle, Henry IV, and his father, Edmund de Langley, held the same appointment to Richard II. It is more than probable, then, that the treatise was the joint production of father and son, and though several writers ascribe its authorship, or translation from the French, to Edmund de Langley, yet one of the manuscripts dedicates the work to Henry IV from " Your owyn in every humble wyse, Edward Plantagenet." Whoever was responsible for its introduction into English, it is apparent that the book is merely a slightly altered translation of Gaston de Foix's *Miroir de Phœbus*, or as it is sometimes entitled, *Livre de Chasse*. The author of this work on field sports in France was a feudal baron living close to the borders of Spain, which lends colour to his contention that Spain was the country of origin of the breed of dog whereof he wrote as follows: " Another manner of hound (the word dog was not then in general use) there is, called hounds for the hawk, and Spaniels, for their kind came from Spain, notwithstanding that there be many in other countries. Such hounds have many good customs and evil. Also a fair hound for the hawk should have a great head, a great body, and be of fair hue, white or 'tavele' (i.e., pied, speckled, or mottled),

2

WOODCOCK SHOOTING

for they be fairest and of such hue they be commonly the best. A good Spaniel should not be too rough, but his tail should be rough. The good qualities that such hounds have be these—they love well their master and follow without losing, although they be in a crowd of men, and commonly they go before their master, running and wagging their tail and raise or start fowl and wild beasts but their right craft is of the partridge and the quail. It is a good thing for a man that hath a noble goshawk or a tiercel or a sparrow hawk for partridge to have such hounds. And also when taught to be 'chien couchant,' they are good to take partridges and quail with the net. And also they are good when they are taught to swim and good for the river, and for fowls when they have dived.''

Another early reference to '' Spanyellys,'' but lacking any description of the dog and his users, occurs in the *Boke of St. Albans* (1486), sometimes termed *The Book of Field Sports*, attributed to Dame Juliana Berners, Prioress of Sopwell Nunnery, Hertfordshire, and published by Winkin de Worde in 1496. Strutt the author of *English Sports and Pastimes*, avers that the *Boke of St. Albans* was compiled from a tract entitled the *Crafte of Huntynge*, by William Twice or Twety, huntsman and '' Maister of Game '' to King Edward II, or from an enlargement made from Twety's tract by Henry IV for the use of his son, Prince Henry. In any case, the St. Albans book is obviously a school book, so written that a pupil whilst learning to read might, at the same time, become acquainted with the names of the animals and phrases used in venery and field sports. There is frequent mention of Spaniels in the household records of Henry VIII, as, for example, that '' Robin, the King's Majesty's Spaniel Keeper,'' was paid a certain sum '' for hair cloth to rub the Spaniels with.''

At that period falconry was the sport of kings and the nobility, but when game was required for food a more speedy method of securing it was necessary. Partridges, quail and pheasants, as well as rabbits and hares, were caught in snares. Netting was introduced and Spaniels were utilised in driving birds towards the fowlers stationed with their extended nets. The idea of drawing the nets towards the dogs and of enclosing them under its meshes

4

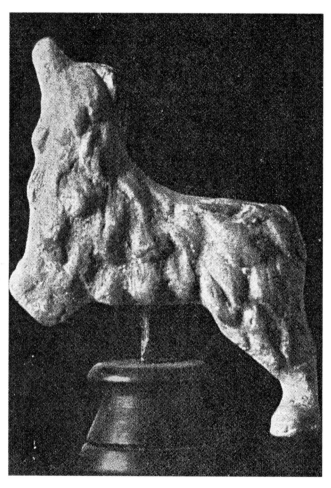

A SMALL DOG IN TERRA COTTA
Having a decided Spaniel-like appearance, Cypriote Collection,
Metropolitan Museum of Art, Central Park, New York.

5

together with the driven birds is said to have originated
with John Dudley, Duke of Northumberland, father of
the famous Robert Dudley, Earl of Leicester. The Duke
was the first sportsman to teach his dogs to sit, or set,
crouching close to the ground for the purpose of allowing
the partridge net to be drawn up to and over them.
The behaviour of the dogs thus broken is described by
Queen Elizabeth's physician, Dr. Johannes Caius, founder
of Caius College, Cambridge. Dr. Caius, at the request of
the naturalist, Conrad Gesner, of Padua (who was occupied
in writing his *Historia Animalium*), penned about 1570
his famous *Treatise of Englishe Dogges, their diversities,
the names, the natures and the properties*. Written in Latin,
this book after the death of Dr. Caius, who was not himself
a sportsman, but gleaned his information chiefly from
the Earl of Leicester and other courtiers and sportsmen
of the period, was translated into English and published
by Abraham Fleming, student, and " Sold by Richard
Johnes over against S. Sepulchre's Church without
Newgate " in 1576. Caius classified all sporting dogs under
two headings, Venatici, which were used for the purpose
of hunting beasts, and Auscupatorii, which served in the
pursuit of fowl. These latter he limited to the " Index or
setter which findeth game on the land," and the Aquaticus,
or spaniell which findeth game on the water." Of these
varieties, termed in Latin Hispaniolus, he says in the
second part of his discourse, " Such dogs as serve for
fowling, there be two sorts. The first findeth game on
the land; the other findeth game on the water. Such as
delight on the land, play their parts, either by swiftness
of foot, or by often questing, to search out and to spying
the bird for further hope of advantage, or else by some
secret sign and privy token betray the place where they
fall. The first kinde of such serve the hawke; the second
kinde serve the net or traine. The first kind have no
peculiar names assigned unto them save only that they
be denominated after the bird which by natural appointment he is allotted to take, for the which consideration,
some be called dogs for the falcon, the pheasant, the
partridge and such like. The common sort of people call
them by one general word, namely, Spaniells. As though
these kind of dogs came originally and first of all out of
Spain, the most part of their skins are white and if they

6

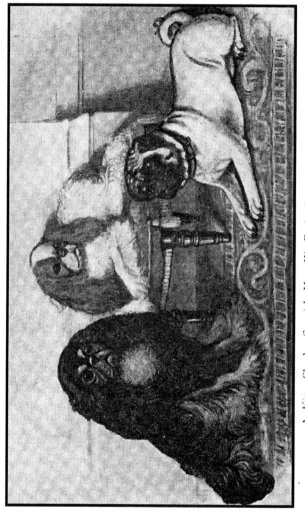

A King Charles Spaniel, Mrs. W. F. Lee's Jules; a Blenheim,
Mrs. W. F. Bagnall's Polo; and a Pug, Miss Barlow's Nicodemus
(from an old coloured print)

7

be marked with any spots, they are commonly red and somewhat great therewithal, the hairs not growing in such thickness but that the mixture of them may easily be perceived. Othersome of them be reddish and blackish, but of that sort there be very few. There is also at this day among us a new kind of dog brought out of France (for we Englishmen are marvellous greedy, gaping gluttons after novelties, and covetous cormorants of things that be seldom, rare, strange, and hard to get); and they be speckled all over with white and black, which mingled colours incline to a marble blue which beautifieth their skins and affordeth a seemly show of comliness."

Were these black Spaniels alluded to by Dr. Caius the progenitors of the present-day Cocker?

It is generally assumed that the Toy Spaniel of the period contemporary with Dr. Caius was of a sturdier, heavier type than the specimens associated with that designation to-day.

At Chatsworth, the Derbyshire seat of the Dukes of Devonshire, there is a painting of Charles II whereon the artist depicts the Merry Monarch with a Spaniel which compares not unfavourably with the modern Cocker. Beyond such fragmentary evidence there is no actual proof in support of the generally accepted contention that the Cocker is a close relative of the original Blenheim Spaniel, nevertheless the writer is prepared to admit, if not to endorse, the correctness of this view, the more so as within the memory of the present generation Blenheims of a distinctly robust type were to be found in the Blenheim and Woodstock districts. These, excepting in head formation, differed very little from the Cocker, and sporting writers of the past century almost unanimously conceded that the Blenheim Spaniel was frequently utilised as a sporting dog.

Nicholas Cox, writing in *The Gentleman's Recreation* in 1677, refers to the land Spaniel as " of a good and nimble size, rather small than gross, and of a courageous mettle; which, though you cannot discern being young, yet you may very well know from a right breed which have been known to be strong, lusty, and nimble rangers, of active feet, wanton tails, and busy nostrils, whose tail was without weariness, their search without changeableness, and whom no delight did transport beyond fear or obedience."

In the *Sportsman's Cabinet*, published in 1803, there is a graphic description of the Spaniel: " The race of dogs passing under the denomination of spaniels are of two kinds, one of which is considerably larger than the other, and are known by the appellation of the springing spaniel —as applicable to every kind of game in every country; the smaller is called the cocker or cocking-spaniel, as being more adapted to covert and woodcock shooting, to which they are more particularly appropriated and by nature seem designed." After referring to " the true English-bred springing spaniel," the author continues: " From this description the cocker differs, having a shorter, more compact form, a rounder head, shorter nose, ears long (and the longer the more admired), the limbs short and strong, the coat more inclined to curl than the springers, is longer, particularly on the tail, which is generally truncated; colour, liver and white, read, red and white, black and white, all liver colour, and not infre-quently black with tanned legs and muzzle. From the great similitude between some of these cockers and the small water-dog, both in figure and disposition, there is little doubt but they may have been originally produced by a cross between the springing spaniel and the latter. Some of the largest and strongest of this description are very common in most parts of Sussex and are called Sussex spaniels. The smallest spaniels passing under the denomination of cockers is that peculiar breed in possession and preservation of the Duke of Marlborough and his friends, these are invariably red and white with very long ears, short noses, and black eyes; they are excellent and indefatigable, being in great estimation with those sports-men who can become possessed of the breed. It is upon record how much that unfortunate monarch Charles I was attached to spaniels, of which he had always favourites about him; and although they were supposed to be of the small, black, curly sort, which bear his name, they were much more likely to have been of the distinct breed of cockers, if judgment may be consistently formed from the pictures of Vandyke, in which they are introduced. The large springing spaniel, and the diminutive cocker,

9

although they vary in size, differ but little in their qualifications except that the former does not equal the latter in the rapidity of action; nor do they seem either to catch the scent so suddenly, or to enjoy it with the same ecstatic enthusiasm when found. The smaller spaniel has also the advantage of getting through the low bushy covert with much less difficulty than the larger spaniel, and in that particular department may probably not tire so soon, whatever may be the length and labour of the day. Spaniels of both descriptions are used as

CHAMPION LILY OBO

finders in coursing with greyhounds, and are eagerly indefatigable in their exertions to find and pursue a hare, as they are in search of winged game with the gun. From the time they are thrown off in the field, as a proof of the pleasure they feel in being employed, the tail is in perpetual motion (which is termed feathering), upon the increasing vibration of which the experienced sportsman well knows when he is getting nearer to the object of attraction. The nearer he approaches the game he is in

10

pursuit of, the more energetic he becomes in his endeavours to succeed; tremulative whimpers escape him as a matter of doubt; but the moment that doubt is dispelled, and the game found, his clamorous raptures break forth in full confirmation of the gratification he receives; and this proclamation may be so firmly relied on (though in the midst of the thickest covert), that the happy owner may exultantly boast he is in possession of at least one faithful domestic who never tells a lie."

Bewick in his *History of Quadrupeds* adds colour to this assumption by his description of the King Charles and Cocker Spaniels. Of the latter variety he wrote: " The

FRED AND CHAMPION OBO

Cocker is lively, active, and pleasant an unwearied pursuer of its game, and very expert in raising woodcocks and snipes from their haunts in woods and marshes, through which it ranges with amazing perseverance. Of the same kind is that beautiful little dog, which in this country is well known under the appellation of King Charles dog; the favourite and constant companion of that monarch, who was generally attended by several of them. It is still preserved as an idle but innocent companion—its long ears, curled hair, and web feet evidently point out its alliance with the more useful and active kind last mentioned."

11

In support of this supposition one may aptly quote that great canine authority, Dr. J. A. Walsh ("Stonehenge" of *The Field*), who wrote: "The Blenheim and King Charles Spaniel will be described under the head of toy dogs, to which purpose alone they are really suited, though sometimes used in covert shooting." The same writer classifies Spaniels in two groups, viz.: (1) "the Springer, including Sussex, Clumber, Norfolk, and local strains; (2) the Cocker, so called from his being chiefly utilised for woodcock shooting, though also good for general purposes. The latter variety is a light, active Spaniel of about 14 lbs. weight on the average, sometimes reaching 20 lbs., with very elegant shapes and a lively and spirited carriage."

Blaine in the *Encyclopædia of Rural Sports* (1840) is credited with the following: "The Cocker, so called from his appropriation to woodcock shooting, has a short, round head when compared with that of a springer; he is, also, much smaller in size, more compact in his frame, and not high on his legs. His ears are usually long and well feathered, as are also his legs and tail, his hair likewise generally is more waved and curled than that of the springer spaniel. The Cocker of the present day is very diversified in his colour, occasionally he is an entire black and then he is indeed a beautiful animal." The same writer referring to the Blenheim Spaniel says, "they were one and all (red and white) zealous hunters in the field, but required much trouble to break," but in alluding to the strain of black and white Cockers for which the late Lord Rivers was celebrated, Blaine says, "these dogs turned out most excellent in the field and were shot to by us with less breaking than any others we ever remember."

Further testimony to the claim of the sporting and toy Spaniels to a common ancestry is adduced by Rawdon B. Lee in his *Modern Dogs*. Referring to land and water Spaniels, Lee wrote, "From these two breeds of Spaniels, I believe, have sprung all the varieties known at the present time, not excluding the toy Spaniel. Writers on canine matters so recently as within the present century, have told us that the Blenheim Spaniel was at that time used for covert shooting and was useful in such a capacity."

It is worthy of note that throughout all these early writings no mention is to be found of the Cocker as a *retrieving* Spaniel. His abilities were almost exclusively employed in pushing out game to the guns in covert shootings and in woodcock hunting.

The late Mr. James Farrow (owner of the celebrated Obo), whose knowledge of Spaniel lore was probably unrivalled, remarks in his monograph on *The Clumber Spaniel* that " the original Blenheim was a sportsman and that it is certain the breed was used as a gundog as well as a companion; and what is more, was built on the lines

CHAMPION TED OBO

for work, much more so than half the Cockers one comes across at our dog shows to-day.''

It is to the Principality of Wales, however, that we owe one of the earliest mentions of the Spaniel as a recognised breed of dog. In the Laws of Howel Dda (obit 948), promulgated fully a century prior to the Norman Conquest, there is a section entitled, " The Worth of Dogs,'' a code setting forth the value of different breeds of dogs, in which the following occurs: " The Spaniel of the King is a pound in value. The Spaniel of an uchelior, a pound. The Spaniel of a free-man is six score pence in value. The Spaniel of an ailt, four pence, the same value as his cur.''

13

The foregoing extracts from the writings of men well qualified to advance opinions from as far back as it is possible to probe into the ancestry of the Cocker Spaniel affords sufficient proof, if such were necessary, that the Cocker or Woodcock Spaniel can claim to rank as a pure breed for more generations than many others of the canine family. It must be recognised, however, that reilable data upon which to connect the present-day Cocker with those utilised by the sporting men of the seventeenth century is lamentably deficient. It can only be surmised that the many hues of our modern Spaniels are attributable to the selective crossing with the original red and white or Blenheim Spaniel. A present-day authority on the breed, Mr. C. A. Phillips, is of the opinion that a close relationship existed between the Field Spaniel and the Cocker. " Stonehenge " described the Welsh and Devonshire Cockers of his time as " both of a deep liver colour," whereas to-day these two varieties are admittedly only recognised as typical when their colourings are red and white.

CHAPTER II

You last thro' the day with your keenness unflagging,
Your nose on the ground, your tail ever wagging;
And you don't seem to care if with bramble and thorn
Your coat and your ears are all tattered and torn.

Brown.

LATER HISTORY

*DIVIDING Line between Cockers and Field Spaniels
—A New Era—The Obos—The Kennel Club and
Cockers—American Cockers and the Obos—The Brutons
—The Rivingtons—Of Wares—Trumpingtons—Brae-
sides — Bowdlers — The Doonys — The Galtrees — The
Rocklyns—The Fulmers—The Pinbrooks—The Fair-
holmes—The Falconers. THE POST-WAR PERIOD:
Dominant Sires—The Bazels and Dunfords—The
Blaedowns—The Byfleets—The Churchdenes—The Cob-
nars—The Conchietons—The Dobrows—The Felbriggs
—Of Fews—The Foxhams—The Glenbervies—The
Gulvals—The Hubbastones—The Melforts—The Otter-
shaws—The Oxshotts—Of Sauls—The Treetops—The
Vivary—Cocker Spaniel Prefixes and Affixes.*

THE dividing line between Cocker Spaniels and Field Spaniels was, up to a few years ago, one of weight only. At dog shows classes were provided for " Field Spaniels over 25 lb." and for " Field Spaniels 25 lb. and under." In both of these classifications the type was identical, and puppies from the same litter were frequently to be seen competing in each division. This hard and fast rule that a Cocker Spaniel should not exceed 25 lb. in weight was far from being in the best interests of the breed. Many specimens of admitted great merit were debarred from competition from the fact that they exceeded by a few ounces the weigh limit imposed. The breed, at this time, was making only small headway, and the Field Spaniel was by far the more popular.

A new era dawned, however, when the Spaniel Club in 1901, by special resolution, abolished the weight limit for

15

Cocker Spaniels, and from that year onwards steady progress has been evinced. Uniformity in type was almost immediately noticeable, and breeders began to produce and exhibit sturdy, short-backed Cockers, scoring heavily in spring of ribs, depth of girth, and activity.

THE "OBOS"

Of the early strains of Cocker Spaniels none achieved more renown and greater distinction than the " Obo " Kennel of Mr. James Farrow. It is not too much to say

that the " Obo " dogs formed the tap-root of the modern Cocker, a contention that all students of pedigreed Spaniels will readily endorse.

In 1870, Mr. Farrow had attained success with a smart little dog named Emperor, but this dog does not figure at all conspicuously in the pedigrees of that period, and the "Obo" strain can be taken as the foundation of this famous kennel. The original Obo, whelped 14th June, 1879, was descended from Cocker Spaniels kept for many years by the late Mr. Burdett, whose black-and-tan, Frank, was mated in the fifties of the past century with a black-and-white bitch, Venus, owned by Mr. Mousley. In the resultant litter was Bob, the

THE LATE MR. J. J. FARROW forerunner of the Cocker Spaniel as we know it on the show bench to-day. Obo's sire was Fred and his dam Betty, both descendants of Mr. Burdett's Spaniels, Fred being a son of Bebb, which in turn owned Old Bebb of Lord Derby's strain as sire.

That great authority on Spaniels, Mr. F. E. Schofield, writes: " Obo, it goes without saying, was the greatest force in the revival of the Cocker, especially in the matter of size, for he and his progeny enabled breeders to utilise Field Spaniels (Springers, as they were then termed) in the certainty that among the offspring there would be many small puppies ideal in size to the Cocker breeder."

In passing, it may be of interest to mention that it is from Alonzo that practically all coloured Cockers are descended. On this point Mr. Schofield writes: " I quite agree that Alonzo may be taken as the foundation-stone for *colour* in Cockers, but I do not think he was in any way responsible for type." Alonzo was a close relative of Obo's and did much, also, to establish colour in the Field Spaniel, a circumstance which proved again that the sole difference between the last-mentioned variety and the Cocker was merely one of weight.

From Obo sprang Champion Lily Obo, a black bitch, afterwards mated to Frank Obo (a grandson of Obo), and the union produced Champion Ted Obo, whose name appears with great frequency in the pedigrees of most black Cockers. The detailed pedigree of Champion Ted Obo is as follows:—

	Frank Obo	Tim Obo by Obo
		Beverley Fan
CH. TED OBO		
	Ch. Lily Obo	Obo
		Gipsy

Writing with reference to this dog, Champion Ted Obo (40,697), Mr. J. Farrow says: " My black Cocker Spaniel, Ch. Ted Obo, was whelped on 25th August, 1894, and was bred by myself. His weight when in show condition was 25 lbs. His dam, Lily Obo, was considered by most of our expert Spaniel judges as the most typical of perfect Cockers ever exhibited. Ted Obo's grandsire, Champion Obo (10,452), was exhibited for eight years at most of the important shows and under as many different Spaniel judges, and never was beaten when exhibited in classes provided for Cocker Spaniels. This dog's stock did so well in America that one hundred guineas was offered by an

American breeder for the use of this Spaniel for one season's stud service. This offer was refused. I have had this kind in my kennels for thirty-four years, and as far back as 1873 won first prize and a special for best small Spaniel or Cocker in the exhibition at a dog show held in the Manchester Free Trade Hall."

Several of the Obo strain were exported to the United States, and for many years their descendants were easily recognisable, both in this country and in America, for their " trueness to type " and likeness to their famed ancestor. Many of the " Obo's " and " Omo's," the productions of modern American kennels, can claim direct descent from Mr. Farrow's dog. According to modern ideas, the chief failings of the Obo type was a tendency to be a trifle full in eye and " too close to ground." However, they were an undoubted step in the right direction. I believe the last brace shown by Mr. Farrow was Bebb Obo and Mary Obo—compact, nicely balanced, well-ribbed up, little dogs with typical heads.

From the details given of later strains it will be noted that almost without exception they all trace descent from the " Obo's." The successes of this kennel attracted many breeders to espouse the Cocker, and Mr. Schofield, Mr. Aynsley, Mr. J. W. Robinson, Mr. Price, Mr. Holley, Mr. C. A. Phillips, and Mr. R. Lloyd were among those who helped to evolve the modern dog from the very scanty material available. Very rarely, in those days, could an all-black litter be counted upon, and at every whelping the puppies were diversified in colouring, liver, liver-and-tan, and black-and-tan predominating, while blue-roans were unknown.

Some interesting details, throwing much enlightenment upon the history of the early strains of Cocker Spaniels, were contributed in 1897 to the canine Press by Mr. James Farrow, who wrote:—

" When staying with poor Phineas Bullock at Bilston for a day or so to talk Spaniels and to have a look around his kennels in 1874, I well remember his telling me that the greatest mistake he ever made was selling a Spaniel named Bebb. It is a strange fact, but nevertheless a true one, that from the first dog show held at Newcastle, in 1859, down to the Birmingham Show of 1896, in a very large number of instances, the most prominent prize-winning Spaniels of the day have not been at the service of the general body of breeders for stud purposes, and no owner that I have ever known was more peculiar in this respect, or more jealous about his Spaniels, and kennel matters generally, than Phineas Bullock, selling very few specimens, and never allowing use of same save only to friends who, from some cause or other, he cared to see and talk with. Some of my friends, who, like myself perhaps have long since swallowed the first issue of the Kennel Club stud book, 1859-74, will perhaps say: 'But if this is so, how is it we see so many dogs bred by Phineas Bullock recorded as winners in the stud book, and owned by Capt. Hon. W. Arbuthnott and Mr. J. Fletcher?' Well, as this is a matter that has nothing to do with the pillars of the stud book, I will leave this point with the remark that I stand to my opinion, and presume that both these exhibitors must have been two of the very few favoured friends of one of the most, if not the most, prominent breeder of Spaniels during the first ten years of dog shows. Now for the Spaniel, Bebb. Why did ' Bullock ' regard the sale of this Spaniel as the mistake of his life in Spaniel matters? For this simple reason: Jealous to an extreme of his beauties, he quickly found he had sold a trump card, and that Bebb was, as a stud dog, open to the world, and as a pillar of the stud book. This Spaniel has not, in my humble opinion, had an equal from the commencement of dog shows up to date. It matters not what prominent Spaniel's pedigree—Field, Cocker, or Sussex—we unravel, Bebb's blood turns up in 80 per cent of them, and he is directly responsible for such champion specimens as Bullock's Bob (2,106). Mr. Spurgin's Christy (2,122), a big winner, and the sire of the Spaniel of all others to this day immortalised by the breeders and exhibitors of Field Spaniels other than black, i.e., Alonzo (2,098). Bruce (2,117), a black dog, second only in his time to Bob (2,106), is another direct son of Bebb; Dash (2,125), another Spaniel in type and quality only a little behind Bruce; George (2,146), a grandson, and entered in the stud book as a Sussex, was a big winner, and this dog led to a great unpleasantness between the then champion of Sussex Spaniels, Mr. Bowes, and Bullock, over a win by this Spaniel at Birmingham in the Sussex

19

Cocker Enthusiasts All

Left to right: Mr. H. S. Lloyd (the Author), Col. Downes-Powell, Mr. C. A. Phillips, the late Mr. R. Somersgill, and Mr. H. Scott

class, in the year 1874; Max (2,149), bred by Mr. Spurgin, and recorded in stud book as a Sussex 'and a dog after the present stamp' of Sussex Spaniel, was a grandson of Bebb; Mass (2,150), bred by Mr. Spurgin, a Cocker, or a winner under 22 lbs., was a grandson of Bebb; Chloe, a 23 lbs. specimen, was another of Bebb's grandchildren and a big winner; Nellie (2,225), a black Spaniel bitch that old Spaniel men are never tired of talking about, a champion of champions in her days, was, perhaps, Bebb's most prominent daughter. It is as well, perhaps, to mention at this stage that in the pedigree in the first volume of the Kennel Club stud book that Mr. Bowes and Mr. Spurgin, in their Spaniel's pedigree, referred to the Bebb I am referring to as 'Bebb', and, perhaps, correctly so; but 'Bullock', in his pedigrees, referred to the Bebb I am speaking of as Young Bebb. The sire of Bebb, the pillar of the stud book, was a Spaniel of 'Bullock's' named Bebb, a dog I never saw. Just to name another well-known Sussex Spaniel of the old school, and allowed to be by some Sussex Spaniel men of that time a typical specimen, was Rex (2,163), a son of Bebb. Bachelor (6,287), a dog that in more recent years played such a prominent part in the Newton Abbot kennel of celebrated black and other Spaniels, was out of Peggie, a direct daughter of Bebb. I have said sufficient, I am sure, to show your readers that Bebb, as a pillar of the stud book in the class of Spaniels known as Field, Cocker, and Sussex, is what I have placed him, a champion of champions; and right glad I am that my old friend Bullock made the mistake of which in after life he so much regretted. Now for a few words about Bebb's points as a Spaniel for the information of your readers who never had the pleasure of seeing the dog. He is entered in the First Vol. of the stud book as a liver-coloured Sussex. Well, as a matter of fact, he was no more a Sussex in type than I am like a black man. Indeed, the only point about him, including pedigree, that could be called Sussex was his colour, and that was far from typical when compared with the colour of the Sussex Spaniels seen to-day. In Bebb's days many Spaniel men called every Spaniel that was liver coloured a Sussex, in the same way as a good number of Spaniel men to-day call all Spaniels under 25 lbs. Cockers. As a Field Spaniel Bebb had really a very grand

21

head, a head that would fit in with the particulars given in the standard of points issued by the Spaniel Club for Field Spaniels as near as any Spaniel dog I know to-day. He had very long ears, too long I used to fancy a little, wonderfully low set, tail action good, with a good body and the best of legs and feet, and a little too much coat; in outline, of course, very different from the typical dog of to-day; nevertheless, what in those days was considered long and low, but when I tell your readers that he weighed in show form 38 lbs. and stood 18½ inches in height, a very poor show, they will at once say, this grand old 'pillar' would make if he could be compared with the long and low celebrities of 1897. When I used Bebb he was the property of that old breeder and exhibitor of Spaniels, Mr. Spurgin, of Northampton, and in those days this gentleman thought, as I did, that when in show form Bebb was invincible.

" I have very little doubt, myself, that the very first Spaniel exhibited that can claim in any way to be fairly typical, and of something like reliable pedigree as a Sussex, was Dr. Salter's Chance (2,119), born 1865, and entered in Vol. I, Kennel Club stud book, as a Sussex, and often quoted in show catalogues as of pure Sussex pedigree. This dog can fairly claim to have been one of the first pillars of this variety of Spaniels, and he did a lot to fix the type at the earlier dog shows. Mr. H. Green's Guess (9,265) and Guy (8,352), two Sussex dogs that did a lot of winning, and a lot to fix Sussex type, were out of Chloe, a bitch of the Chance blood, and a winner. I remember this dog quite well, and although I firmly believe he was as pure in pedigree as could be well obtained in those days, he was not of the type that a few years after we were introduced to as absolutely the pure article in type and pedigree, i.e. Buckingham (4,400). When Buckingham was brought out, a good majority of Spaniel breeders accepted him as the type against the Chance (2,119) stamp, and that view has more or less been carried down to this date. As a sire, Buckingham must also take a prominent place in the building up of our Sussex Spaniels. He was much used at stud, and perhaps his two best sons were Bachelor (6,287) and Rover III (5,249), two dogs that have not only played a prominent part in the pedigrees of a very large number of Sussex Spaniels who have been large winners, but also a large number of our best Field Spaniels, black in colour. I have said of the two types of Sussex originally introduced, the majority of Spaniel men plumped for Buckingham, and I think wisely. No man liked a sporting Spaniel better than the gentleman who introduced us to Chance (2,119), i.e. Dr. Salter; but to take the points of Chance and Buckingham for hard Spaniel work, Buckingham certainly had much the best of it, notwithstanding the fact that I have heard the owner of Chance state that he never owned a better Spaniel for work. Chance had long, heavily-feathered ears, whereas Buckingham had moderately-sized ears, which were not overdone with feather. Chance had too much coat, which at times was curly, whereas Buckingham's coat, although dense, was not long anywhere. Again, Chance's legs were rather heavily feathered, whereas Buckingham had little or no feather on hind legs, and, indeed, what feather he had was of that beautiful quality and quantity that would not hinder him in the roughest of work. We had no classes for Cockers in those days; now and again a show gave a class for Spaniels used for field or covert work, under 25 lbs., which weight at a later date was often reduced to 22 lbs., and in these classes we had simply small Field Spaniels. I remember at Manchester, in 1873, I won first prize and cup for the best Field Spaniel under 25 lbs., used for field or covert purposes, with a little black dog called Emperor, but although he was much shorter in body and longer on leg than many in his class, he certainly was built more on Field Spaniel lines than what we now think a Cocker should be. At the very earliest period of dog shows, Dr. W. W. Boulton, of Beverley, claimed to have a breed of almost pure Cockers, and exhibited them as such, but I always regarded most of them as Springers or Field Spaniels; indeed, Mr. Boulton, to me, started on wrong lines, as from the very earliest days the Cocker has always been admitted to be the smallest class of Spaniel used for sporting purposes, and that this gentleman— although he won a very large number of prizes with his Spaniels—was wrong as to the size of a Cocker is to me most clear, from a letter from his pen which appeared in *The Field* of 25th December, 1869, and which runs as follows: 'Mr. Blades much doubts whether a Cocker can

23

Two Famous Cocker Judges—Mrs. Higgens and Mr. Trimble

24

reach more than 27 lbs. without being crossed. I myself possess a grand young dog between fifteen and sixteen months old of this breed, at the present moment exhibiting at the Manchester Show. This dog really weighs when fat about 35 lbs., and is splendidly made in all points. His measurements in ear, head, etc., are wonderful for so young a dog, and it is a surprise to me that he has been altogether overlooked by the judges.' Many of the small Spaniels, sometimes called Cocker, at the period I have been dealing with in this paper, were by Bebb (2,101), the wonderful sire I have previously referred to, and to get at anything like a pillar of the stud book of our Cockers we must work down to a more recent date.

" The action of the Kennel Club in not acknowledging the Cocker as a distinct variety of Spaniel, so far as requiring a separate position in their stud book and on their register forms, unfortunately kept this variety of Spaniel back for years. I have advocated its cause in this direction through the *Kennel Gazette* and other ways since 1881. The editor of *The Field* kindly backed up my suggestion with the following note *re* this point in *The Field* of 30th December, 1882: 'We have no great fondness generally for particular names, but we quite agree with our correspondent that there is a meaning in the term Cocker which renders it one that it is desirable to retain.'

" At last, with the help of the Spaniel Club, the Kennel Club in 1892 gave the Cocker the position it ought to have had years before in their stud book, and, of course, the interest taken in the breed increased at once, and continues to increase. Owing to this mixing up of the Field Spaniel—large and small—and Cocker, we really do not come to a specimen that may be called a direct sire of Cockers only until about seventeen years ago, and in 1880 I introduced what I honestly and fairly think may claim to be the champion, even to this day, of pillars of the stud book of our Cocker sires. I refer to Champion Obo (10,452). On his sire's side this dog was bred from the Burdett and Bullock strain of Cockers, and on the dam's side from a black-and-tan—to-day's type—of Cocker bitch given to me when a school boy by a sporting friend who resided at Foulsham, in Norfolk, whose family had had the breed for many years, and in those days only those up to a hard day's work and sensible specimens

25

were allowed to live, as absolute sporting purposes were about their only enjoyment and dog shows were hardly heard of. I think, perhaps, in dealing with this dog on paper it would be more agreeable to quote from the canine Press a few remarks—as to his suitability as a sire—when he passed over to the great majority at the good old age of about a dozen years: 'As a sire he excelled any Cocker seen since the history of dog shows. As a prize winner, when exhibited in Cocker classes, he never had his flag lowered, although exhibited for nearly eight years under some different judges. It is as a pillar of the stud brook of the breed that Mr. Farrow thought so much of his old favourite, and to name the numerous prize-winners by this dog would take up too much of our space. Some of the most prominent are Champion Miss Obo (12,745), Champion Jennie Obo (20,655), Champion Lily Obo (29,159), Bob Obo (10,452), Jack Obo (19,253), Gipsy Obo (10,452), Ben Obo (24,771), Dolly Obo (15,841), Keno (16,471), Little Smut (10,452), Tim Obo (29,134), Frank Obo (36,451), etc. We are often told of the grand Cockers seen at American exhibitions, and we wish to take nothing from our friends across the water, but the fact remains that Obo is sire or grandsire of half of their prominent winners, indeed, if one goes through carefully the list of American prize-winning Cockers (writing in 1890) during the last seven years, certainly 75 per cent. of them belong to the Obo strain.'

" Referring to this dog as a sire, I care only to add to the above remarks from the *Stockkeeper* that his position as a sire in the American breed of Cockers refers equally as strongly to the Australian Cockers through his son Jack Obo (19,253).

" A very nice little dog, with a lot of true Cocker type about him, was Little Bob II (12,717), bred by Mr. Freem, of Flint, and whelped in 1880. Although Little Bob never sired anything of the very first water that I remember, he did a lot of good just at this time to fix Cocker type, and was considerably used when the property of Mr. E. C. Holford, the honorary secretary of our first Spaniel Club. On the sire's side, Little Bob was bred from Bullock's Bob, but it was more from the dam's side that Little Bob II got his Cocker points and outline—Busy (10,466). Although, on her sire's side Busy was from large Field

Spaniel stock, her dam, Mag, had the Beverley Cocker blood thick in her veins, and Busy herself was a very compactly-built one (small when compared with her sire), a black-and-tan with the length of leg—not leggy— but just the difference required, and valued by some in those days for marking just the difference in outline between the Springer and the Cocker. Busy was not known much to show-goers, but I remember quite well carefully looking her over after she won the cup for best black-and-tan, or black, white and tan Spaniel, at Birmingham in 1880. A dog that, I think, I ought perhaps to have mentioned previously, if not only for the fact of his being about the first dog, a prominent winner under 25 lbs. weight, entered in the first volume of the Kennel Club stud book, with really some good Cocker points about him, is Nigger (2.153), born in 1869 and bred by Mr. Murchison. He was afterwards owned and exhibited by Mr. R. J. Lloyd-Price and Mr. Shirley, but I do not know if he was used much at stud. Nigger was certainly quite distinct from the Field Spaniels of his day, but his pedigree on the dam's side, I believe, was uncertain. Anyway, it is not given in the first volume of the stud book, but it is a fact that he had a lot of good, sound Cocker points about him, and I often think of this dog when looking at the Cocker dog I am now showing—Champion Ted Obo. They are certainly much alike in expression and other points, and about the same size and height. Keno (16,471), by Champion Obo out of Young Rhea (12,751), bred by Mr. Bond, of Londonderry, was a good stamp of Cocker, and combined the old Beverley and Obo Cocker blood and proved quite a useful sire. In his time good, small Cocker-built dogs were difficult to find. Beverley Rex (20,605) was one of his useful sons; Breda Boy (20,607) another; Beverley Fan (20,641) and Beverley Rhea (20,642) were two more than useful bitches by this dog, and he sired, also, many other good Cockers.

" Bob Obo (18,491) was another useful dog, and sired, in addition to Champion Jennie Obo (20,655), many good specimens, but this dog was not much used in this country; he had not quite the Cocker outline I like. A Cocker called Little Smut (20,619), whelped in 1884, somehow or other made his mark in Cocker history. I bred him, but he was a most miserable specimen, and I sold him, I believe, for

Group—Cocker Club Championship Show, 1933

three guineas for a little house dog. He was an outcross
on dam's side, as an experiment the result of which I
thought nothing of further than always regretted I did
not have him put in the pail early in life with others of
his litter. Ditton Beta (24,813); Brevity (27,017), another
Birmingham winner; Jim Obo (31,469); Ridgeway Raca
(36,465); Rivington Ray (38,690), etc. Toots (31,485), a
Cocker out of a bitch by this dog, Little Smut, has also
a considerable number of winners recorded to him in the
stud book, and some useful specimens, too, such, for
instance, as Trumpington Daisy (40,716), Dolly (40,706),
Bruton Violet (40,702), Ch. Ladas (40,693), Ulster Queen
(38,695), Rathgar Jet (38,687), Bruton Ouida (38,673),
and others. Rivington Signal (29,132), bred by Mr.
Phillips, was a better stamp of Cocker than some of the sires
previously mentioned, and in build was quite after the
stamp of his grandsire, Keno (16,471). This dog has been
considerably used, and has done much good to fix Cocker
type, and has sired no end of useful specimens. Tim Obo
(38,692) is another dog that has left his mark as a sire
in the stud books most strongly.''

THE BRUTONS

This strain, established by the late Mr. C. Caless, was
noted for big bone, perfect coats with excellent feathering,
and depth of brisket. On page 30 is reproduced a photo-
graph of Mr. Caless's original brace of Cocker Spaniels.

Toots	Beverley's Don (20,645)	Keno (16,471)	Obo (10,452)
			Young Rhea (12,757)
	Fan (9,290)	Easten's Busy (14,792)	
Ridgeway Raca	Little Smut (20,169)	Obo (10,452)	
	Dottie	Chelmsford Caution (19,906)	
		Fan VI (12, 735)	

A study of this illustration will well repay, denoting as
it does a type differing in many respects from that of the
ideal Cocker Spaniel of the present day. This brace of

Toots and Ridgeway Raca

dogs, Toots and Ridgeway Raca, both blacks, were the progenitors of the Bruton strain, and it will be of interest to append their pedigrees, showing the " Obo " blood on both sides, though in this instance the influx of Field Spaniel blood will be noted on the female side.

DITTON GAIETY

Fan (9,290) was a pur Cocker, and the dam of several winning coloured dogs, including Ditton Gaiety and Rivington Merrylegs.

Toots was one of the greatest show dogs of his time. He weighed 23 lbs., and is described as " sharp and intelligent, very active, with a good Cocker head, has a good coat, is well feathered, possesses perfectly straight legs, with plenty of bone, is well proportioned, in fact, every inch a Cocker."

From Toots and Ridgeway Raca Mr. Caless bred an ever-improving line of blacks, their immediate progeny including Champion Bruton Floss, which, in turn, produced Bruton Tony. From these came the line of blacks, Champion Bruton Victor, Bruton Gerald, and Bruton Peter. The last named was a son of Victor ex Floss, and was the sire of Bute, which in turn was the sire of Paddy, Ted, and other well-known dogs remembered by breeders and exhibitors in the immediate pre-War days.

FIELD TRIAL CHAMPION RIVINGTON DAZZLE

CHAMPION RIVINGTON ROBENA

THE RIVINGTONS

The originator of the Rivington strain, Mr. C. A. Phillips, can claim to be one of the pioneers in the breed, and his kennel consists of both blacks and coloured. Both colours are descended from Obo stock. A daughter of Obo in Rivington Sloe was the dam of Rivington Signal and Riot; the latter was by Rio, another son of Obo.

Rivington Signal was sired by Breda Boy, a son of Keno and a grandson of Obo. Riot was mated to Rivington Bloom (a daughter of Rivington Signal) and sired Rivington Redcoat, a dog pre-eminent in the breed at that period. Redcoat eventually found his way to France, and there assisted in establishing a successful kennel of Cockers for the late Monsieur Chas. Hazard, a foremost French Breeder. Redcoat subsequently become the property of Mr. R. Lloyd. It is mainly to the careful selection and study of blood lines by the owner of the Rivington prefix that the Cocker possesses the definite and well-established type it does to-day. Mr. Phillips produced champion after champion. In the blacks, he was materially assisted in this through having imported in the early days of his kennel the black dog Toronto. This dog was bred in America, and was a direct descendant of the original Obo. Noteworthy inmates of the Rivington Kennel include Race, Bloom, Dora, Ch. Robena, Ch. Ruth, Ch. Pride, Ch. Rogue, Regent, and Ch. Rivington Reine. The last named was bred by Mr. R. Lloyd, and was a dominant factor in the evolution of the black Cocker, being in herself quite a forerunner of the modern type. Mated to a liver and tan Field Spaniel named Lucky Traveller (then considered an ideal in type), she produced Rivington Arrow. Arrow, in turn, was mated to a black dog, Hampton Guard (an importation from America), the litter resulting in Rivington Rogue, Quiver, Archer, and others whose influence on the breed have been most pronounced. Rivington Rogue, when mated back to Rivington Reine, produced a litter in which was Rivington Regent, a dog far too large for purposes of exhibition, nevertheless a most prepotent sire, his progeny including Galtrees May.

D   33

Without a doubt, Galtrees May was the best black Cocker ever bred up to that time and could hold her own even to-day. Doony Dora and Fairholme Kathleen, the latter a red bitch which achieved a good measure of success at field trials, also in the show ring, were among the same litter by Rivington Regent—Galtrees Nell.

Doony Dora became the dam of Galtrees Raven, a noted black sire. Though, as mentioned, Fairholme Kathleen was quite a successful dog, it cannot be recalled that any of her descendants proved to be exceptional, either at work in the field or on the bench, whereas Galtrees

HAMPTON GUARD (American bred)

Raven left his mark on the breed and among his descendants are counted many of our best Cockers. Another of the same breeding was a liver-coloured, high-quality bitch in Galtrees Flora. Her quality was undeniable, and she did a lot of winning, despite her colour, one which never became fashionable. Had she been a black, she would have equalled her litter sister, Galtrees May. It will be observed that the dam of these two, Galtrees Nell,

Pedigree of

BARNSFORD BRIGADIER (A6)

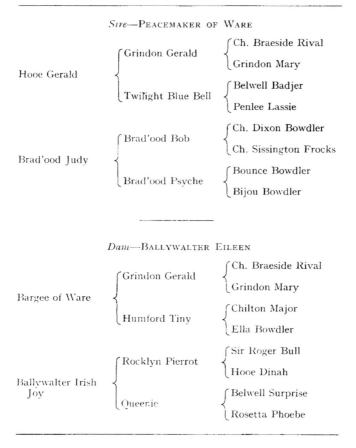

Sire—PEACEMAKER OF WARE

Hooe Gerald
- Grindon Gerald
  - Ch. Braeside Rival
  - Grindon Mary
- Twilight Blue Bell
  - Belwell Badjer
  - Penlee Lassie

Brad'ood Judy
- Brad'ood Bob
  - Ch. Dixon Bowdler
  - Ch. Sissington Frocks
- Brad'ood Psyche
  - Bounce Bowdler
  - Bijou Bowdler

Dam—BALLYWALTER EILEEN

Bargee of Ware
- Grindon Gerald
  - Ch. Braeside Rival
  - Grindon Mary
- Humford Tiny
  - Chilton Major
  - Ella Bowdler

Ballywalter Irish Joy
- Rocklyn Pierrot
  - Sir Roger Bull
  - Hooe Dinah
- Queenie
  - Belwell Surprise
  - Rosetta Phoebe

35

was sired by Hampton Guard, the imported dog, thus two crosses were introduced in three generations. Here is a detailed pedigree of Champion Rivington Rogue.

Pedigree of

CHAMPION RIVINGTON ROGUE (A2).

Sire—HAMPTON GUARD (1)

Hampton Red Lance	Red Diamond	Red Doe
		Queen Ready
	Hampton Jewel	Red Doe
		Nelly Bly
Hampton Yola	Ch. Omo	Ch. Black Duke
		Ch. Baby Ruth
	Hampton Quality	Ch. Omo
		Hampton Jesso

Dam—RIVINGTON ARROW

Lucky Traveller (2)	Kingsley Radiant	Kingsley Bogie
		Kingsley Ayah
	Kingsley Kaga	Coleshill Climax
		Kingsley Sunbeam
Ch. Rivington Reine	Heir Apparent	Craigrowans Heir (3)
		Sceptre
	Cruiskeen	Trumpington Ton
		Hibernia

(1) Pure American blood containing a double cross of Mr. Farrow's Ch. Obo.
(2) Field Spaniel blood.
(3) Sired by Toronto, the imported dog which was strong in Obo blood.

36

BRAESIDE BUSTLE

The first recognised blue roan, founder of the Braeside and Bowdler strains.

Below is appended the pedigrees of Galtrees May, Fairholme Kathleen, Doony Dora, and Galtrees Flora (B.2).

Sire—RIVINGTON REGENT

Ch. Rivington Rogue (1,107N)
- *Hampton Guard (A.K.C. 76,781)
- Rivington Arrow

Ch. Rivington Reine (1,142K)
- Heir Apparent
- Cruiskeen

Dam—GALTREES NELL

*Hampton Guard A.K.C. 76,781)
- Hampton Red Lance (A.K.C. 57,518)
- Hampton Yola (A.K.C. 57,520)

Julia of Ware
- Master Gilbert (1,432F)
- Julian

* Imported.

37

THE "OF WARES"

The late Mr. R. Lloyd, who was a contemporary of Mr. James Farrow as a breeder of Cocker Spaniels, founded this strain as far back as 1875. At that time the affix ' of Ware '' had not been adopted. This was introduced by the author, who carried on the kennel on the death of his father. With very scanty material available, the late Mr. R. Lloyd eventually built up a strain composed chiefly of black and tans and liver and tans. He had acquired several Cockers of these two colourings from a

HEIR APPARENT
(Black)

Mr. Holley (previously mentioned), and the pedigrees of these acquisitions dated back on the female side direct to the Beverley strain through Champion Fop and Alonzo, thence to the Bullock strain. Of this blood was Little Prince, sire of Champion Crown Prince, both bred by Mr. R. Lloyd. Crown Prince, a small liver-and-tan dog, had a very successful bench career, and from him sprang Regis II, an undoubted factor in fixing the Doony Cockers. Little Prince, a black, tan, and white, was the sire of Myrtle, from whose union with Mr. J. W. Robinson's black Cocker, Rio (by Champion Obo ex Tyneside Fancy,

Pedigree of
CHAMPION INVADER OF WARE (Blue Roan) (A.8)

Sire—Drumraney Gunner
(Brother to Nominee of Ware)

Fairholme Rally
{ Belwell Swell
{ Carrybridge Reminder

Ballywalter Lady in Blue
{ Rocklyn Pierrett
{ Queenie

Dam—Drumraney Wonder

Barnsford Brigadier
{ Peacemaker of Ware
{ Ballywalter Eileen

Arabian Meg
{ Algy of St. Foy
{ Arabian Joyce

RADIUM OF WARE (*a pre-war Championship Winner*)

the latter a liver roan), the late Mr Lloyd bred a liver-coloured bitch, afterwards named Braeside Bizz. Bizz was mated to his black dog Viceroy (sired by Toots), and when in whelp was purchased by Mr. J. M. Porter, who from this litter, and particularly from the blue roan dog, Braeside Bustle, whose full pedigree appears on page 45, laid the foundations of the Braeside strain.

A remarkable feature of this dog, Braeside Bustle, was his propensity for transmitting his colouring of blue roan to his progeny. Invariably, the puppies sired by him—and he was in great demand as a stud dog—partook of the same colouring, yet a research into his pedigree fails to disclose any ancestor of a similar colour, or to adduce any reason to account for the circumstance. His litter brother, a black and white, named Brother Sam, was never able to reproduce this blue roan colour, at that time greatly desired by breeders.

Shortly after this period a black dog, Heir Apparent, whose name appears in the detailed pedigree of Champion Rivington Rogue, was bred by Mr. R. Lloyd, and sired by Craigowan's Heir (by Toronto) ex Sceptre (the latter by Trumpington Tony ex Hibernia by Champion Ted Obo.) Heir Apparent had a great stud career, siring among many others such well-known Cockers as Champions Doony Blackie, Dusk, Rivington Reine, Belwell Squire, Rock Girl, and Rock Heiress.

Pedigree of

WHOOPEE OF WARE (K.C.S.B. 453 MM) (A.9)

Sire—CH. CHURCHDENE INVADER
(Brother to Wildflower of Ware, the dam of Luckystar of Ware.)

Ch. Invader of Ware	Drumraney Gunner
	Drumraney Wonder
Blue Rocket	Rocklyn Merryman
	Miss Dolly Blue

Dam—FOXHAM MINX

(Dam of Ch. Blanche of Ware, Vivid of Ware, Violet Ray of Ware, etc.)

Corn Crake
{ Dyrons Blue Coat
{ Rocklyn Betsy

Foxham Magpie
{ Fulmer Ben
{ Blue Tit

Photo   PEACEMAKER OF WARE   [*Hedges*
(Blue Roan)

From this time onwards the affix " of Ware " was attached to the kennel, and the successes of its inmates belong to contemporary annals. Mention might be made, though, of some of the outstanding winners belonging to this kennel. These include Champion Invader of Ware, Champion Irresistible of Ware, Champion Clarion, Champion Evermerry, Champion Exquisite, Champion Wiseacre, Champion Magnetic, Radium, Raven, Guard,

41

Champion Truth, Joyful Joe, Irrepressible, Lovable, Champion Blanche, Champion Homespun, Champion Umpire, Champion Eloquence, Champion Inspiration, etc. Since this work was first written others which have upheld its traditions are Luckystar of Ware, which created a unique record by twice having been acclaimed Champion of Champions at Cruft's, the world's greatest show, in two successive years. This dog has also been awarded on thirty-four occasions the coveted award of best all breeds in show. Field Trial Cocker Championship Stakes have also been won by this kennel

INVADER OF WARE, WHOOPEE OF WARE, LUCKYSTAR OF WARE

with Field Trial Champion Tornado (sired by Champion Invader of Ware), Field Trial Champion Barney and Field Trial Champion Tiptoe. Of even more recent date Whoopee of Ware, the blue roan, for he, it is claimed, has created a world's record by winning 54 challenge certificates, and as a sire stands alone to-day, his most outstanding daughter being Exquisite Model of Ware, which has not only collected 47 challenge certificates in a very brief space of time, but secured the " blue ribbon " of the canine world by being acclaimed the supreme champion of the world's greatest shows—Cruft's, 1938 and 1939, and the

42

Kennel Club, 1938. Silver Templa of Ware is another multiple championship winner who was placed reserve for a similar honour in 1937; he has left a lasting impression on the breed, and in Australia is sure to prove an invaluable stud force. Manxman of Ware did much to carry on the good work, and his son, Sir Galahad of Ware, is considered by his owner the best dog he ever owned. It will be of interest, too, to note that following the precedent established by Toronto and Hampton Guard, the " of

CH. INVADER OF WARE
(Blue Roan)

Ware " kennel has had recourse to the imported Canadian Cocker, Broadcaster, for new blood to assist the black variety. Broadcaster is a direct descendant of the famous Obo, and his progenitors were American bred for thirty years. Another American was Robinhurst of Ware, and more recently an imported black bitch, My Own Charm, from a famous American strain. It is interesting to note what a prominent part these imported sires have played in producing the reds and goldens.

THE BRAESIDES

The kennel of coloured Cockers known by the prefix of
" Braeside " was established by Mr. J. M. Porter, and
had as its foundation the liver and white bitch, Millstone
Duchess, from which most of the modern coloured ones
trace descent.   Duchess produced Champion Braeside
Betty, and this bitch was mated to Braeside Bustle
(aforementioned).   The union resulted in a litter of which
Blue Peter was the most noteworthy.   The influence of
this dog in fixing and transmitting the characteristics of

J. M. Porter, Esq.
(" Braeside ")
One of the founders of the Cocker Spaniel Club.

44

the coloured variety has been most marked and will endure for many generations. John Bull, the progenitor of the tri-colours, was one of his sons, and sired, in turn, Champion Rivington Ruth and other champions.

Another son of Braeside Bustle was Champion Ben Bowdler; indeed, there are very few of the coloured Cockers that cannot trace back to this wonderful sire, Braeside Bustle.

It is greatly to be regretted that Mr. Porter has not maintained his interest in the breed.

The following is the pedigree of Braeside Bustle:—

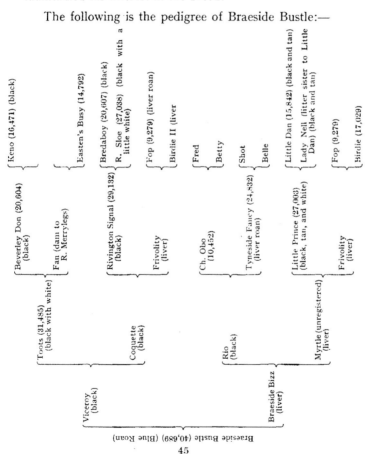

THE BOWDLERS

In the history of the Cocker Spaniel no kennel has
achieved greater success than the Bowler affix of Mr.
R. de C. Peele, who produced champion after champion
with monotonous regularity.

MR. R. DE C. PEELE ("Bowdler")
One of the founders of the Cocker Spaniel Club

In February, 1906, Mr. R. de C. Peele, writing in *Our
Dogs*, says:—

    " I purchased my first Cocker at Leominster
Show in 1892, and registered her as Batchcott Rose

(black). Mated with Tim Obo (black), she bred
Bess Bowdler (black and tan), 1893, my first winner.
This bitch, bred to her father, produced Rose
Bowdler (black) (1894) who in turn mated with
Bruton Don (black) bred Phyllis Bowdler (black,
1896). Mated to Braeside Bob (lemon and white),
bred Judy Bowdler (black and tan, 1898), who
mated with the two sires I then owned, Blue Peter
(blue roan) and Ben Bowdler (blue roan), bred me

CH. JETSAM BOWDLER
(Black)

respectively Champion Rufus Bowdler (red) and
Juno Bowdler (black and tan, 1900), and Champion
Bob Bowdler (blue roan, 1901).

" Students of pedigree will find that our modern
Cockers are almost entirely the result of the patience
and skill of Messrs. Aynsley, Caless, Farrow, Lloyd,
Price, Phillips, and Robinson."

The foregoing is of interest in showing that a humble
start by a determined and careful student met with the
greatest possible success.

CHAMPION BOB BOWDLER

CHAMPION BEN, CHAMPION BOB AND CHAMPION DIXON BOWDLER.

Ch. Ben Bowdler, a son of Braeside Bustle, was the sire of Ch. Bob Bowdler ex Judy Bowdler. The last-named bitch was also mated at a later date to Blue Peter, and was the dam of Ch. Rufus Bowdler, which, in turn, sired three champions, viz.: Ch. Braeside Rival, Ch. Truth, and Ch. Chilverton Patsy. Ch. Ben Bowdler was the sire of two noted champions, viz.: Bob Bowdler and Doony Swell. The former was the sire of Ch. Dixon Bowdler, which had an unbeaten show record, while Doony Swell also assisted in carrying on the strain, being the sire of at least one champion. Ch. Dixon Bowdler was generally considered the best blue roan ever seen up to this time, and it is doubtful if a more typical Cocker has been whelped. Another to add lustre to the kennel was the black, Ch. Jetsam Bowdler (the dam of Ch. Jock Bowdler). Curiously enough from " Jetsam " and " Jock," her son, there appears few outstanding descendants of this line to-day. This bitch may be taken as the forerunner of the existing type of black Cocker; she was most compact in body, unexcelled in neck and shoulders, and with the exception of a light eye could more than have held her own in the keenest competition in the show ring to-day.

Mention should be made, too, of Ch. Susan Bowdler, a liver roan and tan of Braeside blood, and a noted bench winner.

In a letter dated February, 1931, Mr. R. de C. Peele, communicating with the author, writes:

" I always think your father responsible for the modern type of Cocker being shown. If he had not given Jetsam Bowdler the championship at Cruft's, no one else would have had the pluck to break away from the type then winning.

" It created a sensation at the time, but she never looked back and won under all judges consistently."

As recently as January of 1939 the same great authority writes:—

" I have seen lately dogs which may not be really great, but which I know could have won all before them in pre-War days."

This tribute to the modern Cocker from such a source is praise indeed.

THE TRUMPINGTONS

During the past decade, much spade-work towards establishing the Cocker Spaniel, particularly the black variety, was achieved by the late Mr. T. Harrington under the prefix of "Trumpington." His kennel was founded on Obo and Bruton blood, and produced many good and typical specimens of the breed, including Champion Trumpington Daisy (by Toots ex Trumpington Gem). A son of Daisy's, called Trumpington Tony, proved a corner stone to the breed and was responsible for many winners. Among his progeny were many prolific bitches, which proved of inestimable value as brood matrons to their fortunate owners. One of his sons was the celebrated Champion Trumpington Ted.

In addition to Cockers, the breeding of the coloured variety of Field Spaniel claimed much of Mr. Harrington's attention, notable productions of this latter variety emanating from the kennel, including that good brace, Champions Trumpington Dora and Roger, and other pillars of the stud book.

THE "DOONY'S"

MR. E. C. SPENCER'S COCKERS
Champions Doony Blackie, Betty, Swell, and Bess

From stock of Ch. Obo origin Mr. E. C. Spencer evolved this successful strain. His Doony Regis II, when mated to Braeside Sam, a descendant of Braeside Bustle, bred Ch. Dooney Belle, one with an unparalleled career of success at shows. Belle changed ownership on several occasions, and apparently left no progeny of note, but her sister, Doony Flirt, when mated to Ch. Ben Bowdler, produced a prepotent blue roan in Ch. Doony Swell. Swell had great influence on type in the years immediately prior to the great war. He also was remarkable for the working qualities he transmitted to his descendants.

Turning his attention to the black variety, Mr. Spencer bred Ch. Doony Blackie and Ch. Doony Dusk, both sired by Heir Apparent ex Doony Pride. This brace brought into prominence the results of a combination of Obo blood and that of the same strain reinfused through the imported and American-bred Cocker, Toronto.

THE GALTREES

Although not a distinct strain, it is only fitting that some reference should be made to the dogs bred by Mr. J. Sowray during his brief association with Cocker Spaniel-

---

Pedigree of
GALTREES RAVEN and CH. HAMPTON MARQUIS (A.4)

Sire—ARLINGTON MARQUIS

Verrell of St. Foy	{ Arabian Bute
	{ Peggy Miller
Winifred of St. Foy	{ Woden Sportsman
	{ Harmony of St. Foy

Dam—DOONY DORA

Rivington Regent	{ Ch. Rivington Rogue
	{ Ch. Rivington Reine
Galtrees Nell	{ Hampton Guard
	{ Julia of Ware

51

GALTREES RAVEN
(Black)

GALTREES MAY
(Black)

52

dom. The descent of Galtrees May, Galtrees Flora, Raven, Fairholme Kathleen, and others have been previously noted, and from this Galtrees blood sprang Hampton Marquis and Galtrees Raven (through Doony Dora, a sister to Galtrees May). From Marquis and Raven can be directly traced many of the superlative qualities possessed by the " Pinbrooks " and " Fulmers."

From a combination of the Galtrees and Hampton Guard blood several pure whites were produced, which, in the opinion of the writer, goes to prove that " pure whites " can *only* be produced from solid coloured specimens, and not from parti-colours.

THE ROCKLYNS

Mr. F. C. Dickinson, the owner of the Rocklyn prefix, has bred many high-class Cocker Spaniels, and it was a matter of universal regret when his kennel was reduced to a minimum. Among the black variety, probably his

Pedigree of

ROCKLYN MAGIC (B.4)

Sire—ROCKLYN RAJAH

McCura Dhuv	{ Brunswick Darkie
	Warburton Lily
Rocklyn Ruth	{ Ch. Jock Bowdler
	Hyndburn Beauty

Dam—DUNKELD COMET

Ch. Rivington Rogue	{ Hampton Guard
	Rivington Arrow
Murrayfield Kit	{ Braeside Brush
	Princess Maisie

ROCKLYN MAGIC
(Black)

SOUTHERNWOOD CRITIC
(Blue Roan)
Supreme Champion of Kennel Club Show

54

best specimen was Rocklyn Magic, sired by Rocklyn Rajah, the latter a son of McCaura Dhuv by Brunswick Darkie. To Magic belongs the distinction of a definite type, one greatly in vogue prior to and in the immediate post-war period. Few of the black variety now to be met with are entirely devoid of Rocklyn blood. Magic was bred by Mr. H. Haxton, but early in his career found a new master in the owner of his sire. He came out at Taunton, and the second time he was exhibited won the challenge certificate and a round dozen of first prizes, and shortly afterwards was acquired by Mr. R. de C. Peele, who disposed of him to Mr. Daniels, of Hillingdon. In 1918 a further transfer was effected, and he became the property of Miss Lloyd, joining the " of Ware " stud.

With a combination of Braeside and Bowdler strains, Mr. Dickinson evolved some beautiful specimens of the coloured variety, including the founder of the Fairholme kennel in Carrybridge Reminder, which was bred from Rocklyn Roza. Southernwood Critic, as an inmate of the Rocklyn kennel, created a record for the breed by on two occasions winning the cup for best dog of all breeds at the Kennel Club Show, and by winning outright the Cocker Club cup, which had to be won three times, in the keenest competition of the year. Many other famous Cockers bore the " Rocklyn " hall-mark, and the annals of Cockers are strewn with their influence.

THE FULMERS

The late Mr. Ralph Fytche evinced an interest in Cockers during his undergraduate days, when he became the possessor of one of the breed purchased from the late Mr. Charles Lawrence, of Chesterton. The pedigree of this acquisition, I believe, goes back to Mr. John Smith's " Coleshill " strain. It is recalled that this bitch was a black and white and that it was mated to Byford Baron. From this union sprang the nucleus of the Fulmer strain. It was not, however, until shortly before the outbreak of the war (1914) that Mrs. Fytche established the Fulmer kennel as it is known to-day. Subsequent purchases of,

FULMER BEN

CHAMPION PINBROOK SCAMP

among others, Beau Bowdler, Sherington Fashion, and Ch. Hampton Marquis, were further stepping-stones to the unqualified successes Mrs. Fytche has attained in the Cocker world. Celebrated inmates of the Fulmer kennel were Ch. Fulmer Peat, Maxim, Kaffir, Gleam, Spot, Countess, Bustle, not overlooking the claims to prominence of Fulmer Ben, a dog which achieved a record for the breed to that date by winning no fewer than twenty challenge certificates, and later Fulmer Peggy's Pride, etc.

THE PINBROOKS

Largely built on the Galtrees strain, which harks back to the Rivingtons, the Pinbrook kennel, owned by the late Mr. W. H. Edwards, is noted for its red Cockers, also for the amount of bone and substance they possess. One of the most successful dogs from this kennel, Ch. Pinbrook Scamp, a descendant of Galtrees Raven (see page 56), was a black, however, and had the distinction of being for many years the only champion in the breed. Others to mention are Pinbrook Rufus, Marcus, Amber, and Sand Boy, while Monkerton Charlie, a black and tan of rare quality and a descendant likewise from the Galtrees, has every right to be termed one of the Pinbrooks.

THE FAIRHOLMES

Mr. F. Gordon George, when purchasing the blue roan bitch, Carrybridge Reminder, by Ch. Belwell Surprise, displayed excellent judgment; even so, he could have had at the time but small conception of the ultimate worth of his acquisition or of the great value she would eventually become to the breed. Mated on several occasions to Belwell Swell (by Byford Baron ex Durban Dinah), Carrybridge Reminder has in successive litters produced some of the outstanding coloured specimens and innumerable winners. Ch. Doony Bluebell, Fairholme Trusty, Type, and Typist, are notable, while the blue roan, Fairholme Rally, has attained conspicuous success as a field trialler, and at stud was responsible for transmitting length of head, then much needed in the breed, and sired innumerable winners.

Pedigree of

FAIRHOLME RALLY (169T) (Blue Roan) (A.3)

Breeder: Mr. Gordon George   Born 14th December, 1912

Belwell Swell
- Byford Baron
  - Ch. Doony Swell
  - Byford Betty
- Belwell Rattle
  - Ch. Dixon Bowdler
  - Fan Bowdler 211 M

Carrybridge Reminder
- Ch. Belwell Surprise
  - Arabian Sam
  - Arab Floss
- Rocklyn Roza
  - Carrybridge Bramble
  - Carrybridge Navato

Full brother to Fairholme Type, Trusty, Ringlet, Typist and Ch. Doony Bluebell

Sire of Drumraney Gunner, through whom comes Ch. Invader of Ware, Vivary Crusader, Churchleigh Stormer, Ch. Churchdene Invader, Whoopee of Ware, Exquisite Model of Ware, Manxman of Ware.

Sire of Fulmer Ben, from whom comes Ch. L'ile Beau Brummel, Rufton Rally, etc.

Sire of Falconer's Spangle, from whom comes Cobnar Critic, Joyful Joe, Luckystar of Ware.

Sire of Langmoor Flora, through whom comes Langmoor Vexation and thence Ch. Foxham Migrant.

Sire of Freelance of Ware, from whom comes Lovable of Ware, Ch. Exquisite of Ware, and thence Falconer's Cowslip, and practically all the succeeding "Falconers."

Sire of Rocklyn Merryman, from whom came Blue Rocket, thence Ch. Churchdene Invader, Wildflower of Ware and Lucky Star of Ware.

Sire of Ch. Dazzle of Dunkery, and Daphne of Dunkery, from whom comes Rocklyn Algie, thence Piethorne Jerry, Fulmer Peggy's Pride and Radiator of Solway.

THE "FALCONERS"

Mrs. Jamieson Higgens has ever been essentially a breeder of repute, her experience extending in many directions; Smooth Collies and even cats shared her activities at one time. But the Cocker Spaniel gained pride of place and it is many years ago that the Falconers' strain was established with, I believe, Falconers Business as the first matron of importance to figure in the line; this bitch mated

Pedigree of

SIR GALAHAD OF WARE (C.1)

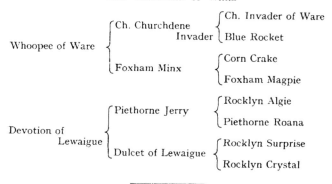

Sire—MANXMAN OF WARE

Whoopee of Ware
- Ch. Churchdene Invader
  - Ch. Invader of Ware
  - Blue Rocket
- Foxham Minx
  - Corn Crake
  - Foxham Magpie

Devotion of Lewaigue
- Piethorne Jerry
  - Rocklyn Algie
  - Piethorne Roana
- Dulcet of Lewaigue
  - Rocklyn Surprise
  - Rocklyn Crystal

Dam—FALCONERS CONFIDENCE

Silver Flare of Ware
- Deebanks Marcus
  - Southernwood Critic
  - Inquisitive Floss
- Baxter Betty
  - Cooleen Dandy Boy
  - Joyce of Blackdown

Falconers Caution
- Cobnar Critic
  - Southernwood Critic
  - Falconers Spangle
- Falconers Cowslip
  - Ch. Invader of Ware
  - Ch. Exquisite of Ware

A Team of "Falconers"
Coloured Cockers

Photo] Grindon Gerald [*Hedges. Lytham*
(Blue Roan)
Pre-war.

to Beechgrove Dandy (a son of Ch. Doony Swell and Ch. Rivington Ruth), her female line being Falconers Bustle and her daughter Rhoda; from the latter mated to Bargee of Ware, sprang Falconers Tidy, Falconers Spangle, Cobnar Critic, Joyful Joe, Luckystar of Ware, etc.

Another daughter of Rhoda—Cinders—in union with Rocklyn Spark, heralded another line which were the forerunners of the Langmoors, Turbarys, etc. But the pur-

FALCONERS COWSLIP
(A famous Matron, Black, White, and Tan)

chase of Falconers Cowslip (by Ch. Invader of Ware ex Ch. Exquisite of Ware) laid the foundation of a line of blood mingling with Silver Flare of Ware and Cobnar Critic, which has generation after generation produced some of the finest bitches yet seen, including Confidence, Careful, Chita, Caution, etc. From this line descends Sir Galahad of Ware.

THE POST-WAR PERIOD

With the almost total suspension of breeding activities during the Great War period (1914-1919) breeders had a very uphill task to re-establish the breed, but they are deserving of the greatest praise and admiration for their efforts, as with the very scanty material to hand in the course of a very few years the Cocker was flourishing more than ever and had gained its present popularity by peaceful methods, by steady progress, and did not burst on the world with a flourish of trumpets, but step by step consolidating its position steadily as it went along.

As this work is intended primarily for the novice and newcomer to the breed it may not be out of place here to reprint an article by the author which appeared in the " Midland Cocker Club's Year Book " for 1938. For the permission to do this the writer thanks the Club.

DOMINANT SIRES

RIVINGTON ROGUE and ROCKLYN MAGIC

Nothing is more interesting to a student of a breed than to endeavour to trace back to where the influence of a particular line of blood or strain emanated, and for the purpose of this brief survey it is unnecessary to go back beyond the immediate pre-war days.

Starting with blacks, Rocklyn Magic, born just prior to the war, had a greater influence on them than any other, and his influence is easily traced back to Rivington Rogue, his dam's sire, who, to students of pedigree, is one of the most interestingly bred blacks of any period. His sire, Hampton Guard, was a solid colour-bred black imported from America, having no English blood in his veins until one gets back to the dark ages of the original Obo, belonging to the late Mr. J. J. Farrow.

Doubtless this dog influenced the tightening up in back and improved the spring of ribs, but it is here suggested that Rivington Rogue's dam, by name Rivington Arrow, had even greater effect on making a lasting impression on successive generations. Arrow's sire, Lucky Traveller, was a liver and tan " misfit " Field Spaniel, being far too short in back and higher on the leg than was considered fashionable in those days. His blood lines traced directly back to all the best Fields of that era, and at no period have Spaniels possessed more wonderful heads or expression.

Arrow's dam, Champion Rivington Reine, was by Heir Apparent, a grandson of another imported Cocker,

FAIRHOLME RALLY at 8 months

Toronto, who traced directly back to Obo—and Reine's dam, Cruiskeen, was also a grand-daughter of Obo.

It will be seen that although many breeders were apt to describe Magic blood as 100 per cent. black, this statement

FAIRHOLME RALLY at 11 years of age

is hardly correct, as through Lucky Traveller is introduced a very strong influx of coloured blood. Curiously enough it is from this " mixture " that all the present-day solid coloured ones owe allegiance.

Galtrees Raven, another grandson of Rivington Rogue, carried on the " influence," his grandson Champion Pinbrook Scamp in turn again linked up successfully the Rogue influence. A great-grandson of Magic, Dominorum D'Arcy, who on his sire's side—Corn Crake was thus 50 per cent. colour bred, can be described as the real ' king-pin " of the blacks since the war. His grandson, on his maternal side, Bazel Otto, proving a successful " carrier " of this influence, amongst his progeny being Treetops Treasure Trove, who in her turn has worthily played her part in maintaining the tradition.

FREELANCE OF WARE
(Blue Roan)

All this brings us back to an appreciation of what we owe to the old-time breeders who had ever an eye on " perpetuity," and with that in their minds they built up slowly but surely, their brains having produced the right material with latent prepotent powers condensed therein for us to carry on with.

Incidentally, the first Kennel Club Championship Field Trial for Cockers was won by the grandson of Rocklyn Magic in Field Trial Champion Ellibank Attention, who in turn has had a very lasting effect on present-day workers.

CORN CRAKE and FAIRHOLME RALLY

In coloured Cockers the two dogs, Corn Crake and Fairholme Rally, whose influence was most felt after the war, and without these two stalwarts Cocker history would have been written on very different lines.

Corn Crake, born in Ireland of English parentage, was a tower of strength, and a search through modern pedigrees will quickly convince those with eyes to see and understand what the present generation owes to his fortunate birth.

Pedigree of

CORN CRAKE (A.7)

Sire—DYRONS BLUE COAT

Rivington Trick
- Fielding Blue Boy
  - Ch. Rufus Bowdler
  - Warburton Blue Bell
- Ch. Rivington Ruth
  - John Bull
  - Rivington Dora

Lady Lamona
- Belwell Swell
  - Byford Baron
  - Belwell Rattle
- Dyrons Beauty
  - Beechgrove Dandy
  - Nurscombe Betty

Dam—ROCKLYN BETSY

Rocklyn Jerry
- Handforth Bang
  - Blackley Rufus
  - Byford Bryn
- Handforth Judy
  - John Bowdler
  - Handforth Shiela

Rocklyn Moormaid
- Ch. Belwell Surprise
  - Arabian Sam
  - Arabian Floss
- Rocklyn Roza
  - Carrybridge Bramble
  - Carrybridge Navako

descending on his sire's side from the Rivington and Bowdler blood, through his tail female line he goes back to solid coloured lines through the late Mr. Trinder's Arabian blood and that of the Bruton-cum-Obo strains.

From Corn Crake descended Southernwood Critic, Cobnar Critic, Foxham Min, Silver Flare of Ware, and many others whose influence has had such a lasting effect on to-day's dogs.

CORN CRAKE

Fairholme Rally, another blue roan, probably had an even greater say in affairs, many of the famous sires and dams of to-day being impregnated with his definite prepotency. Through his son, Freelance of Ware, came Exquisite of Ware, thence Falconers Cowslip, the fount from which the majority of the " Falconers " descend; Falconers Spangle, a daughter, produced Cobnar Critic, which in turn was responsible for Joyful Joe, the sire of Luckystar. Another outstanding son was Fulmer Ben, and from him came L'ile Beau Brummel. Dumraney Gunner, another son, goes down to history as the parent of the immortal Champion Invader of Ware, whose son, Champion Churchdene Invader, carried on the good work in producing amongst numerous others Whoopee, whose progeny are known to all.

From the foregoing it will be seen that the " key " dogs in each generation, although few, have had the prepotency right along the line and the breed has been built up on a comparatively small number, which definitely accounts for the trueness of type existing in Cockers as contrasted to many other breeds.

LUCKYSTAR OF WARE
(Blue Roan)
Supreme Champion of Cruft's, 1930 and 1931

Never let it be overlooked that a sire does not become a stud force of lasting effect by pure chance or accident; the accumulated close ancestors are the people who have most say in the matter, and a careful survey of the pedigrees of the outstanding individuals, matrons and sires of the post-war period will convince any student that " blood lines " are the only royal road to success.

It is of interest to note that Bargee of Ware, a gift to the writer by Mr. J. W. Robinson, a great Spaniel authority of the nineties, was mated to only three or four bitches, yet so dominant is his influence that traceable to him direct are Rivington Dazzle (a powerful and predominant sire in the Field Trial world), Ch. Invader of Ware, and one side of the Falconers' strain.

BAZEL OTTO
(Black)

In this edition it has been felt advisable to give several pedigrees of " key " sires *in extenso*. This will probably be appreciated by the beginner, and in referring to these dogs by numbers and initial letters much reiteration of pedigrees will be avoided.

It is hardly correct to write of the post-war kennels under the heading of separate strains, as during recent years these have become very much more intermingled than was the case in pre-war days. Many causes can be found for this— easier transport, greater opportunities and facilities for getting to shows and seeing the outstanding dogs and bitches, the power of the Press (which through giving greater attention to good production of photographs, articles and other means have educated the average new breeder to a higher standard than was possible before). The various outstanding prefixes of recent years will be dealt with alphabetically and referred to the lines of blood they have been built on by the method referred to. Reference can then be made to the extended pedigrees to see the strains they have been built up on.

THE "BAZELS" AND "DUNFORDS"

Owned by Mrs. J. C. Allan (better known by her maiden name of Miss Taylor) and Mr. Chas. Taylor, built on the Ottershaw and D'Arcy (A.5) blood, produced many good ones, including Ch. Dunford Joy (black), her sister Judy

Photo]   [Fall
BAZEL SOVEREIGN

(black), dam of Bazel Otto (black), Dauntless (black), etc., Bazel Sovereign (red), and many others, Otto having a great influence on succeeding generations.

THE "BLAEDOWNS"

Owned by Mr. J. C. Stone, built up on Hampton Marquis (A.4) blood lines, combined with Ottershaws for solid colours and A.3 and A.7 for the parti-colours. Many beautiful Blaedowns have been benched over a long period of years.

THE "BYFLEETS"

Mrs. M. K. Acton was amongst the first to realise the great future for reds and goldens, and bred many beautiful specimens, Ch. Stardust of Byfleet, Cleo of Byfleet, Lodestar of Sorrelsun, and innumerable others. The " Sauls " line of blood, combined with " Ottershaw " and infusions of imported dogs, together with " of Ware " blood lines, made up the successful " Byfleets."

THE CHURCHDENES

Mr. J. Hough had a brilliant though all too brief career in the breed, building up his kennel on Corn Crake (A.7.)

Photo]   CH. CHURCHDENE CINDERELLA   [Hedges, Lytham
(Blue Roan)

and Ch. Invader of Ware (A.8) infusions. His beautiful Ch. Churchdene Invader, one of the greatest stud forces of all times, was responsible for Whoopee of Ware, and Churchdene Invader's sister, Wildflower of Ware, was the dam of Luckystar of Ware. Churchdene Cinderella, Churchdene Invaderlike, and others all did much for the breed.

THE "COBNARS"

Mr. Colin V. Barraclough has been breeding for many years. A relative of Mr. F. C. Dickinson, he has always had a great liking for a good one, and has owned and bred many good ones—Rocklyn Nib, Mercury, Dusk and

COBNAR CRITIC
(Blue Roan)

Elegance, all names to conjure with in their day. Elegance mated to Dusk produced that outstanding black dog, Truant of Wyming Brook. Cobnar Critic (Southernwood Critic ex Falconers Spangle) goes down to history as a corner-stone of the breed; amongst his most outstanding progeny were Joyful Joe (sire of Luckystar of Ware), Cobnar Frost (himself a great sire), winner of many challenge certificates, Cobnar Pip (a New Zealand champion), and that wonderful team of bitches, Falconers Chance, Caution, Caraway, Contrast, Cora, Credit, etc., all claimed Critic as sire. The history of the breed might conceivably have been differently written had it not been for Cobnar Critic (A.7).

THE "CONCHIETONS"

Perhaps not as well known to the exhibition world as amongst purely shooting and field trial men, yet Mr. R. Carson must have bred as many field trial champions as almost any man. Built up on Bowdler and Rivington blood lines, Ch. Rivington Simon stands out as one of the greatest exponents of Cocker work. Nearly all the Conchie-

F.T. Ch. Rivington Simon

Winner of the K.C. Field Trial Championship

tons have been disposed of and have come into the hands of enthusiasts who have exploited them under their own prefixes.

THE "DOBROWS"

Mrs. A. A. Taylor has played a leading hand in the coloured variety. The names of the outstanding inmates of the kennel that come prominently to mind are Dobrow Dash (a famous sire, claiming many certificate winners as his progeny); Duke, with an equally outstanding record as a sire, also had the distinction of being adjudged the best of breed at the Cocker Club's Championship Show; followed the next year by yet another Dobrow in Decora, who put up a similar outstanding performance; Dobrow Diamond won many certificates, and hosts of others from this mint have won the highest honours throughout the world. Built largely on the A.8 and A.7 lines the kennel has indeed prospered.

DOBROW DIAMOND
(Blue Roan)

THE "FELBRIGGS"

Mrs. Shirres has been one of those quiet breeders who have done much for the breed and produced many specimens without the public realising how much she has really done. Ch. L'ile Beau Brummel probably fills the bill as the best she has ever bred. This black and white had a great career and left his mark, particularly in the North. Felbrigg Bruce, the black, was another outstanding dog whose influence is still felt, and Hortensia, the dam of Treetops Treasure Trove, will go down to history as one of the prepotent matrons of recent years.

"OF FEWS"

From a very modest start with the bitch Jigs, Dr. W. J. Dawson built up a kennel of working Cockers equalled by few and excelled by none. Jigs descended from a strong line of Braesides and Bowdlers and was definitely an Irish product in the later generations. Mated to the Doctor's Gift of Ware (F.T. Ch. Rivington Dazzle ex Torment of Ware), Jigs produced two trial champions, Danseuse of Fews and Sans Petronella; the former has a niche of fame all her own in having produced F.T. Ch. Pat of Chrishull (sire of ten field trial champions).

F.T. Champions Dusk of Fews and Jazz of Fews

Amongst the working champions that this " of Fews " kennel has been responsible for are Jigtime, Jazz, Dusk, Tango, Taffy, Colleen, Gigolo and Flush of Fews, whilst many more descended from arteries of this blood.

THE FOXHAMS

Since the war few breeders have gained greater prominence than Mr. F. W. Bloxham, who built up his kennel on the collective blood of Fairholme Rally (A.3) and Corn Crake (A.7). To enumerate the innumerable

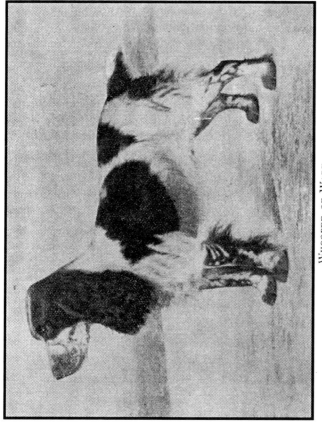

WHOOPEE OF WARE
(Blue Roan)

outstanding dogs bred here space forbids. Foxham Minx must, however, take pride of place as the dam of Whoopee of Ware and Foxham Midas, sired by Ch. Churchdene Invader, her previous litter by Ch. Invader of Ware producing Ch. Blanche of Ware, which for Monsieur C. Daniel Lacombe in France did yeoman service. Emslea Cornflower, Foxham Maypole and Magpie were bitches of outstanding prepotence, and one cannot overlook the claims of Ch. Foxham Migrant, whose name will go down to posterity as a sire of unusual ability. Jane of Hubbastone was another exceptional matron in this kennel.

THE "GLENBERVIES"

Mr. A. Badenach-Nicolson has bred many high-class ones, and others bearing his prefix have had great success

Photo]   *[Adams*

CH. MARKSMAN OF GLENBERVIE
(Black)

both on the bench and as progenitors. Ch. Marksman of Glenbervie, Ch. Horseshoe Primula, Ch. Stardust of Byfleet, and many others have all helped to maintain the high standard the owner of this kennel insists on.

CH. MARKSMAN OF GLENBERVIE and CH. HORSESHOE PRIMULA

THE "GULVALS"

Mr. H. J. Eakers has, as the breeder of the Gulvals, done much in the West of England for the breed; his Gulval Bluebell was quite one of the nicest blues of her period. Bon-Bon, a dog which had a great influence as a sire; Sunflower, a striking orange and white, and hosts of others, have all played their part in upholding the breed's high tradition.

THE "HUBBASTONES"

Mr. C. C. D. Youings has for many years been breeding, blacks being the original colour favoured, fame coming in pre-war years with Exmoor Bloom, which unless memory fails me was afterwards transferred to Lorna Countess Howe and, I believe, was the first Spaniel ever exhibited by Her Ladyship.

Many good coloured ones have since been produced, but the seal of fame was put on the breeding efforts when, after obtaining from the Foxham kennel the bitch, Jane of Hubbastone, this bitch mated to Whoopee produced the all-conquering peerless Exquisite Model of Ware.

77

Photo]   [Fall

¶ EXQUISITE MODEL OF WARE
(Black, White, and Tan)

Supreme Champion Kennel Club and Cruft's Show 1938 and
Cruft's 1939, etc.

THE "MELFORTS"

An Irish kennel of eminence, owned by Mr. W.
McCausland, which has played a leading part in sustaining
the high standard of the breed in a country which has
produced many of the best. Melfort Magpie, a glorious
black and white, herself an outstandingly successful winner,
produced many great dogs, including Melfort Marksman,
Musketeer, Mutineer, and others. Others owned by this

78

kennel were Ch. Foxham Migrant (formerly Melfort Migrant), Manxman of Ware (late Melfort Manxman), M. Mistletoe (dam of Ch. Golfhill Eclipse), Ch. Melfort Melda, dam of Regis of Akron, and scores of others.

Photo]   MANXMAN OF WARE   [*Fall*
(Blue Roan)

THE "OTTERSHAWS"

Primarily interesting himself in blacks and reds, Mr. W. S. Hunt has for a very long period bred many of the best of these colours, and numbers of kennels have obtained foundation stock from here. Ottershaw Marquis (an A.4 dog) was one of the founders of the kennel, to be followed by scores of others whose successes are contemporary history. Ch. Ottershaw Pimpernel stands out as one of the pillars of the red variety, whilst the numbers of both blacks and reds which have obtained the highest honours at all the leading shows have rarely, if ever, been equalled by other breeders.

THE "OXSHOTTS"

Mrs. F. R. Fryer established a prepotent line of blacks, concentrating particularly on blacks, and her D'Arcya, Felsia, and Tallina have reached the highest pinnacle of fame. For years now winner after winner on exactly the same symmetrical lines have made their appearance, all scoring particularly in coat and expression. Derived from A.4, B.4 and A.5 lines.

Pedigree of
DOMINORUM D'ARCY (A.5)

Sire—CORN CRAKE

Dyrons Blue Coat	Rivington Trick	Fielding Blue Boy
		Ch. Rivington Ruth
	Lady Lamona	Belwell Swell
		Dyrons Beauty
Rocklyn Betsy	Rocklyn Jerry	Handforth Bang
		Handforth Judy
	Rocklyn Moormaid	Ch. Belwell Surprise
		Rocklyn Roza

Dam—DOMINORUM DIANA

Driver of Ware	Volunteer of Ware	Galtrees Raven
		Engadine Darkie
	Bruton Dora	Brunswick Darike
		Bruton Judy
Dominorum Dacia	Rocklyn Magic	Rocklyn Rajah
		Dunkeld Comet
	Hoyland Nell	Ottershaw Magic
		Molesey Bess

Photo]   DOMINORUM D'ARCY   [*Fall*
(Black)

THE "OF SAULS"

Although not now actively interested as a breeder, Mrs. J. E. Sothern for a long period produced numbers of the very best blacks, including Helen's Heiress, Gloria of Sauls, Ladye, Dame, Beauty's Girl, and others, not forgetting Rufus of Sauls, a red which did so much to raise the standard of the reds of his period. Two (by Otto) exported from this kennel became champions in America—Ch. Sinner and Ch. Saint of Sauls.

THE "TREETOPS"

It has been given to few who enter the Cocker ranks to build up a reputation as a breeder as rapidly as befell Mrs. de Casembroot, whose first efforts were made as recently as 1932, acquiring at the age of six weeks the black bitch afterwards known as Treetops Treasure Trove from Mrs. Shirres. This bitch, a daughter of Bazel Otto and Felbrigg Hortensia, laid the foundation of a famous family. Mated to the red dog, Woodcock Ringleader, Treasure Trove produced Talkie, one of the outstanding stud forces of his period. Tristan, the red, a son of Otto (A.5) and Treetops True Love, by Gold Standard of Ware, made a great

G   81

COCKERS, "CHANCELLOR OF THE EXCHEQUER."
MR. H. SCOTT, Treasurer of the Cocker Spaniel Club with CH.
VIVARY CRACKSMAN

impression on the reds. Then from Terrific and Temptress came Turtle Dove, winner of several challenge certificates. Tenor, Trivet, Treasury, Trippett and hosts of others have more or less monopolised the awards in the black and red sections during the last few years.

TREETOPS TALKIE
(Black)

THE "VIVARY"

Mrs. Winnie Clark (née Miss W. Scott) has had a long association with the breed, as her father, Mr. Harry Scott, has bred and owned many outstanding specimens, most notable of all being Vivary Crusader, coming from the A.8 family. Crusader's spectacular wins did much to focus attention on the breed, and as a sire he was equally successful. Ch. Vivary Cracksman was another coloured dog of great merit. Ch. Dazzle of Dunkerry, Daphne of Dunkerry, and many others have all had a lasting influence on the fortunes of the Cocker.

The above by no means exhausts the innumerable kennels which have all played their part in continuing the traditions which were set at so high a standard by pre-war breeders and the pioneers. To those who have been omitted by oversight the author's apologies are herewith tendered.

83

COCKER SPANIEL PREFIXES AND AFFIXES AS SHOWN IN THE KENNEL CLUB

ABERTHAW:	J. Thaw.
ALDINGTON:	The Hon. Mrs. E. K. Salmond.
ALVERSTOKE:	Lt.-Col. J. Kyffin.
ALWINTON:	Miss M. Trobe.
ANSLOW:	The Hon. H. Moseley.
APPLEHAY:	J. Hayes.
APPLETIME:	Mrs. Standish King.
ARABIAN:	E. E. Todd.
ARDSDOWN:	J. Lee.
BAZEL:	Mrs. J. C. Allan.
BELLEWARDE:	Mrs. H. O. Wiley.
BERGAMS:	Mrs. B. Stevenson.
BLACKCOCK:	Dr. J. Roche.
BLACKDOWN:	Brig.-Gen. E. B. Wilkinson.
BLAEDOWN:	J. Stone.
BLETCHINGLEY:	Mrs. F. C. Riley.
BONNY MOOR:	T. H. Egglestone.
BOWDLER:	R. de C. Peele.
BRECKONHILL:	G. Curle.
BRECONSIDE:	C. Cleeberg.
BRIARHOLME:	Mrs. M. S. Hobbs.
BRODICK CASTLE:	The Duchess of Montrose.
BROOKHURST:	Miss J. Earwaker.
BROOMLEAF:	Mrs. K. Doxford.
BROWSTER:	Major G. S. Nelson-Scott, O.B.E.
BRYNFUL:	Dr. D. Fulton and Mrs. E. Gorner.
BUNGALOW:	Mrs. H. Simms.
BURNSCOURT:	Mrs. A. W. Dods.
BURNLANE:	R. M. Stevens.
BURPHAM:	Mrs. D. Wolseley.
BYFLEET:	Mrs. M. K. Acton.
CARRAMORE:	Miss D. Hardy.
CARWAYE:	Mrs. B. H. Carr.
CASSA:	Mrs. R. P. Kershaw.
CHELMSFORD:	H. Haylock.
CHILTONFOLIAT:	The Hon. Lady Ward.
CHRISHALL:	J. Kent.
CHURCHDENE:	H. Hough.
CHURCHLEIGH:	Capt. Thorley.
CLONLEE:	D. O. Perry.

COAT HEY:	Mrs. A. Phillips.
COBNAR:	C. V. Barraclough.
COLINETTE:	C. Griffiths.
COLMERE:	Miss W. R. Booth.
CONCHIETON:	R. Carson.
COOLEEN:	Mrs. Laurie and Capt. J. E. McTaggart.
COPPLESTONE:	Miss Y. Street.

NENE VALLEY SAINFOIN
(Red)

CORRAN:	Lt.-Col. W. D. Allan.
COSHQUIN:	W. Shannon.
D'AGOULT:	Mrs. I'Anson-Anson.
DALSHANGAN:	A. L. Trotter.
DATCHWORTH:	Miss M. E. Medley.
DAVECOURT:	Mrs. D. C. Lloyd.

DEEBANKS:	W. Machin.
DEEPDENE:	The Misses Willmore.
DELLCROFT:	Mrs. L. Childs.
DERI:	Mrs. A. S. Brooksbank.
DOBROW:	Mrs. A. A. Taylor.
DOMINORUM:	Leopold Harvey.
EXEVALE:	Miss S. Stoyel and F. Wellington.
FAIRHOLME:	F. G. George.
FAIRLYN:	Mrs. B. Fairweather.
FAIRWICK:	Miss B. A. Clift.
FALCONERS:	Mrs. H. Jamieson Higgens.

SULLA CHIEFTAIN
(Blue Roan)

FELBRIGG:	Mrs. A. O. Shirres.
"OF FEWS":	Dr. W. J. Dawson.
FETHERSTON:	Mrs. B. Fetherstonhaugh-Frampton.
FEWS:	Dr. W. J. Dawson.
FINESHADE:	Miss R. Monckton.
FIVE DIAMONDS:	Miss H. T. Tetley.
FORSBROOK:	G. W. Harris.
FOXBURY:	Col. W. F. S. Casson, D.S.O.
FOXHAM:	F. W. Bloxham.
FRESHWINDS:	Miss S. Phillips.
FULMER:	Mrs. G. Fytche.

FURZEHILL:	Miss H. Grewcock.
GARNES:	A. G. Dickinson.
GLEN:	Mrs. Stonhouse-Williams.
GLENBERVIE:	A. Badenach-Nicolson.
GOLFHILL:	Mrs. Alexander.
GORSELAND:	Miss V. M. Oldham.
GREENELM:	Mrs. N. Hayman.
GREYCLOUGH:	H. Rhodes.
GULVAL:	H. J. Eakers.
HALFORD:	Mrs. A. E. Smith.
HARLEY:	S. F. Topott.

Photo] MASTERMAN OF WARE [*Fall*
(Black)

HARLOW:	Mrs. Illingworth.
HAYGROVE:	H. T. Davis.
HEYDOWN:	Miss M. Carnegie.
HILLINGTON:	Miss P. ffolkes.
HOLMBUSH:	Mrs. A. M. Mallam.
HORSESHOE:	Mrs. M. E. Sadler.
HOUGOUMONT:	Mrs. W. A. Berry.
HUBBASTONE:	C. C. D. Youings.
IDE:	J. H. J. Braddon.
INNHARMONY:	Mrs. C. F. Matthews.

JIND:	H.H. the Maharajah of Jind.
JOYMOUNT:	J. McCartney.
KEMPSTON:	Miss C. Fuller.
KILRUSH:	Mesdames Harman and Duncan.
LICK BLA:	Miss D. M. Fagan.
LIGHTWATER:	Mrs. B. P. Sutton.
LINTHURST:	H. W. James.
LINTONHOLME:	Mrs. W. Watmough.
LOFIELD:	Mrs. Hinds Duffield.
MALWA:	H.H. the Maharaja Dhiraj of Patiala.
MATFORD:	E. Trimble.
MELFORT:	W. McCausland.
MEROK:	Mrs. McKinney.

HEAD STUDY
(American Bred)

MISBOURNE:	Mrs. M. C. Hahn.
MOUNTWILLIAM:	Mrs. W. Waddington.
NENE VALLEY:	Mrs. R. George.
OTTERSHAW:	W. S. Hunt.
OVERDALE:	Mrs. J. G. Abell.
OXSHOTT:	Mrs. G. R. Fryer.
PADSON:	Mrs. Spencer Youlden and Miss M. Stubberfield.
PALOMINE:	Mrs. C. N. Corlett.
PENRHOS:	W. Shingler.
PERSHORE:	Mrs. A. Long.
RAEGILL:	T. G. Handley.
RELWOF:	Capt. E. S. Fowler.

RESOLIS:	Miss K. Shaw Mackenzie.
RHOSWELL:	C. Jenkins.
RICKMANS:	Mrs. J. Verner.
RIONY:	Capt. R. Bacchus, R.N.
RIVINGTON:	C. A. Phillips.
ROSEMOUNT:	E. E. Lindsay.
RUFTON:	R. Cornthwaite.
RYDAL:	W. B. Oldfield.
SANDPITS:	Mrs. P. Price.

Photo]   [Hedges, Lytham

LANEHEAD TRADITION

SHEPPERTON:	J. Hunt Hickin.
"OF SAULS":	Mrs. J. Sothern.
SHERINGTON:	F. A. Hickson.
SILVERLANDS:	Mrs. V. Berdoe Wilkinson.
SIX SHOT:	Mrs. V. Lucas-Lucas.
SMEADS:	H. H. Hore.
SOLWAY:	R. Grierson.
SORRELSON:	Mrs. J. M. Sharman.

STAINLESS:	H. Webb.
SUDDON:	Mrs. A. H. Vesey.
SULLA:	Miss N. McSulley.
SUNKIST:	Mr. D. Mackenzie.
SWINBROOK:	L. H. Hodgson.
TREETOPS:	Mrs. W. de Casembroot.
ULWELL:	Mrs. D. Garrington.
VIVARY:	Mrs. J. H. Clark.
WALDIFF:	Mrs. S. Shakespeare.
"OF WARE":	H. S. Lloyd.
WOLVERSHILL:	G. H. Rumsey.
WYMING BROOK:	A. Reaney.
YOREDALE:	C. C. Forrester Addie.
YSTWYTH:	T. C. Jones.

CHAMPION IDAHURST BELLE

(American bred)

90

CHAPTER III

You tracked that cock pheasant right down the hedgerow,
No matter he's fast, you're a bit slow,
He couldn't escape from your wonderful nose,
Though he objected—he finally rose.

Brown

THE FOUNDATION OF A KENNEL

PITFALLS for the Novice—Size of the Desired Kennel—The Brood Bitch as a Start—Purchasing a Puppy—The Glamour of a Prize Winner—Delusive Advertisements—Essentials for Breeding—Points to Avoid—Situation of the Kennel—Sleeping Accommodation—Design in Kennels—Cleanliness—Construction of Kennels—Sleeping Benches—Roofing—Shelter from Wind—Kennel Management—Worming the Brood Bitch—Worm Remedies—Disinfectants—Grooming—Beds—Meat Rations Essential—Times of Feeding—Vegetables—Puppy Rearing—Variations of Diet—Weaning—Artificial Heat—Treating Puppies for Worms—Puppies out at Walk—Preparing for Exhibition—Teaching Ringcraft—Muscular Development—The Coat and its Care—Trimming—Washing—Etiquette of the Show Ring—Don'ts for Exhibitors.

THE novice who aspires to make a success of his hobby will naturally have first to consider the foundation stock for his kennel. In most cases this means purchasing, and here, at the very outset, he is confronted with numerous pitfalls. He will be well advised to study the breed from every available angle, both by attending shows and by intercourse with owners and breeders of experience and repute. Experienced breeders are, as a rule, only too pleased to help the novice and to give information and advice. The beginner usually brings an abundance of enthusiasm in his self-imposed task. He plunges in, possibly intending to acquire a first-class stud dog, and emerges, probably, with a fifth-rate brood bitch or a litter of nondescript puppies which he has been cajoled into purchasing.

Before acquiring the inmates for his kennel, the beginner should first decide the size of the kennel, that is, the number of dogs he intends to maintain. Then, when he does make a start, let it be on a small scale, acquiring not more than one-fourth of the number which the kennel will eventually accommodate. He should never buy a stud dog until the kennel is an assured success, but had better begin with a young brood bitch. The price of a good stud dog is always high and in the hands of a novice will not earn anything near the amount in stud fees that he would in the more capable hands of the older-established and more practised breeder. Again, after the first generation

Head as seen from the Front

the progeny will be half-brothers and sisters, thus to avoid the dangers of too much in-breeding the novice will have to seek recourse to new blood, entailing an outlay for stud fees.

A maiden bitch may prove to be a difficult whelper, an indifferent mother, or even sterile, and for these reasons alone a *proved* brood bitch will be found to be a much better investment. Preference should be given to one that has breen bred from when young; bitches not bred from until their fourth to eighth season frequently tend to become irregular breeders. It is advisable to make a start with a bitch which has not had more than three litters and one that has successfully reared a goodly proportion of puppies. If the novice does not know the parents or grandparents of the bitch, it is a good plan, if at all feasible, to inspect these. He will thus be able to note if they combine or possess the qualities he desires to have reproduced in the progeny. It should be remembered that a really good brood bitch capable of winning on the show bench, and purchased at £30 to £40, comes far cheaper and will prove more profitable in the long run than three mediocre ones at £10 each. Do not let the glamour of "umpteen " prizes won by the parents carry too much weight; such a record of show bench winnings is merely a guide up to a certain point. When those prizes were awarded the competition may not have been of the keenest, and the inexperienced, through a limited acquaintance of the relative values attached to the wins,

Wrong head, narrow muzzle, and wrong ear placement

may be easily led astray. The canine Press frequently contains advertisements such as: " Pedigree has eighteen champions," " Puppies from prize-winning parents," " Certain to make champions," etc. Few, even among the most experienced of breeders, are able to prophesy with such a degree of certainty, and those of repute do not care to jeopardise the reputation of their kennels by such misleading announcements. The description and standard of points as laid down by the Cocker Spaniel Club (*vide* page 94) should be carefully studied, and with this ideal in mind the novice cannot go far wrong.

It cannot be too strongly emphasised that this standard was not haphazardly drawn up or compiled, but is the outcome of the experience and careful co-operation of generations of breeders, whose aims and objects were solely to produce a dog of the type, characteristics, and abilities for performing the work for which he was intended.

The essential points that the brood bitch should possess may be summed up as:—

(1) Youth and an approximation to the desired type.
(2) Stamina and health.
(3) Substance and size, combined with quality, although many small particularly typical ones have bred many of the best.
(4) Character and a merry disposition.
(5) Free from an exaggeration, with no outstanding fault.
(6) Heart room and well-ribbed body, with powerful quarters and a free, active movement.
(7) Maternal instinct. (In Cockers this will be found to be strongly developed in certain strains or families.)

The points to be most carefully avoided are, in the order of their importance:—

(1) The weedy type of poor constitution.
(2) Light bone.
(3) Unlevel mouth.
(4) Bad pasterns and feet.
(5) Undesirable character or disposition, i.e. combative tendencies.
(6) Old age.
(7) Flat ribs or sides, narrow chest, high tail carriage, and unduly light eyes.

THE SITUATION OF THE KENNEL

This is a matter of greater importance than the beginner usually attaches to it. Environment plays an important part in the development of all live stock and none the less in the case of kennel stock. Contented inmates are always the most profitable. If the kennel is situate in the country where fields, open space, or an expanse of grass is available for exercising purposes, the results will generally be healthy stock, with work reduced to a minimum. Though, on the other hand, the city dweller has the advantage of nearness to market and greater convenience when attending shows, the drawbacks to keeping a kennel of dogs in towns are many and varied. A good working Cocker is not so much at home in our crowded thoroughfares; he resents the lead or chain at first, but soon becomes reconciled, and judging from the condition of the dogs kept in town the life does not harm him. Once, however, having tasted the sweets of country life and inhaled the odour of game he is never so happy as when bustling through the coverts or merrily hunting the hedgerow.

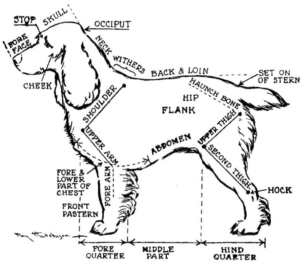

Points of a Cocker

Of course, it is not within the power of all dog owners to let their animals spend their days in the spinneys and plantations, by the water side or in the marshes, but whatever the breed of dog, one thing is absolutely essential, and this is proper sleeping accommodation. If health, strength and condition are to be maintained, then the dog must be free from damp, draughty, and unsuitable sleeping places. It would be difficult to imagine, for instance, a more inappropriate shelter for a dog than the old-fashioned one of a barrel, to which the animal is attached by a short chain. A veritable death-trap, too, is the kennel with a large aperture for ingress and egress occupying almost the whole of the front. Such a den permits the cold winds and rains to penetrate to the furthest corner and is conducive to pneumonia and other ills, affording practically no shelter for the shivering inmate.

The kennel should neither have an easterly or unsheltered aspect, nor a damp foundation. Sunlight, a dry atmosphere, and good air are essential to health and good spirits in the canine as well as in the human subject.

Correct Back and Correct Shoulders

Kennels vary immensely in design. Many of the portable type marketed by the well-known canine appliance manufacturers are admirably adapted to the purposes to which they are devoted. In this matter, as in the acquisition of his stock, the beginner will be well repaid by a visit to any of the widely-known kennels of experienced owners. The questions of drainage, ventilation, aspect, and such-like matters are all points to be noted. Cleanliness, too, should not be overlooked, and the design adopted should be one capable of being kept clean with the least expenditure of labour and time. As regards the construction of the kennel, it should be mentioned that whatever material the floors are made of, they should be quite smooth, if possible with a gentle slope, so that for cleansing purposes the water may run off. Brick paving is porous, and unless the bricks are very evenly laid water accumulates and does not drain off as it should. Boards, likewise, are open to the objection of absorbing moisture, though with care and attention to drying, a boarded floor provides the warmest of all, and if kept covered with coarse sawdust or peat moss, is by far the

Correct Pad   Splay Foot and Pad

best. Concrete is very cold and many cases of kennel lameness, also chills and other disorders, are attributable to its use. Asphalt is preferable, but in the heat of summer is apt to become soft, while stone paving or flagstones are more costly and little better than concrete.

A raised wooden bench should always be provided for each dog to sleep upon. This should be at least a foot

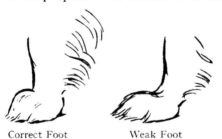

Correct Foot   Weak Foot

above the floor, in order that the occupant escapes all draughts. In the case of pregnant bitches a special bench or box should be supplied, and a description of one suitable for the purpose will be found in the chapter on Breeding. It will facilitate the cleaning process if this bench is portable and easily removed, and there should be a strip of wood about five to six inches wide fastened along its edges to prevent the bedding from falling out.

For roofing, slates and tiles, though expensive, will be found the best. If well laid they are weatherproof, warm in winter, and cool in summer. Thatch is admirable for a roof covering, but is open to the objection that it harbours insects. Corrugated iron is the worst possible material for kennel roofing; it is unbearably hot in summer and the reverse in winter. Match boarding when covered with tarred felt or other roofing material is both economical and efficient.

The fencing to enclose the run or exercise yard surrounding the kennel should always be of such a height that the dog cannot jump over. Care should be taken that no sharp points project upon which the animal might injure itself,

Correct Tail, showing carriage and set on

and it is a good plan to board off, or place a sheet of corrugated iron horizontally along the bottom. This will provide shelter from cold winds and fights between inmates of adjoining kennels will be prevented.

WORMING THE BROOD BITCHES

The brood bitch should be carefully treated for worms. " Stonehenge," in his *Book on the Dog*, says: " Worms are a fertile source of disease amongst dogs, destroying more puppies than distemper itself." There can be no doubt that the reason most members of the canine race are infested with worms is in consequence of its being their nature to eat anything in the form of flesh, i.e. raw liver, entrails of poultry, etc., that is uncooked or partially decomposed. These contain the larvæ or eggs of the different parasites to which the dog is subject, and when swallowed uncooked develop into worms. Their presence causes the animal a good deal of suffering at times, and invariably affects its health, coat, and general condition. There are several varieties of worms found in the dog; the maw worm, the round worm (*Ascaris marginata*), and the tape form are the most common. The last-named usually inhabits the bowels, while the maw worm, which resembles grains of rice and is in reality particles of the tape worm, is to be found inhabiting the rectum. The tape worm resembles a long piece of whitish-coloured tape, with a diamond-shaped head, and until the latter is ejected the dog cannot be considered as freed from the objectionable parasite. The common round worm is of a

Wrong set and wrong carriage

creamy white colour, the female adult measuring from five to six inches and the male, when fully grown, from two to three inches in length. They are to be found in dogs of all ages, and it is among puppies that they do the most mischief. When the loss of flesh or skin troubles— otherwise unaccounted for—a staring coat and a general air of languor and discomfort are evidenced, the presence of worms should be suspected, and prompt measures taken to deal with these pests. The most common and one of the most efficacious remedies for worms is a preparation of freshly-grated areca nut, and the usual dose is two grains for every pound the dog weighs. Santonine, administered in doses from one-eighth to half a grain, according to the size of the dog, should be combined with a purgative, such as castor oil, or 20 to 30 grains of aloes, if it is to prove effective. Turpentine, kamala, Indian pink and oil of male fern are also used as remedies, but the novice will be well advised to confine himself to using either areca nut or santonine, or, better still, to any of the well-known preparations obtainable from those firms who deal specially in canine requisites. It occasionally happens that a vermifuge found to be quite successful in the case of one dog will fail to have the desired effect upon another, and should no results be forthcoming it must not be concluded that the dog is free

| Correct Hocks and | Cow Hocks |
| Hindquarters | narrow Hindquarters |

from worms, but recourse should be had to a second remedy.

The animal should be fasted before administering the preparation, and a good method to adopt is to feed the bitch, say, at mid-day, then about 6 p.m. give a mild dose of castor-oil. Do not feed again, and about 8 a.m. the following morning give (for an adult dog) two tea-spoonfuls of gin in a tablespoonful of milk, followed about thirty minutes afterwards with a quarter of a teaspoonful of *freshly-ground* areca nut in a dessert-spoonful of olive oil. Repeat this dose an hour later and at the expiration of a second hour give a tablespoonful of olive oil. When half an hour has elapsed, a bowlful of warm, sloppy food may be given to the bitch, and she should then be taken for a sharp, short walk. It has been found from experience that the best results have been achieved by halving the dose of the vermifuge and allowing an hour's interval between the two doses. If the full amount is administered in one dose, the bitch will probably eject the lot by vomiting, as the stomach refuses to retain the quantity, but the method suggested gets over the difficulty.

It has been truly said that a man may be a very good judge of a dog, yet know next to nothing of the management of a kennel. To succeed in dog-breeding it is essential to acquire a good knowledge of all matters relating to this subject. For instance, to condition a dog either for exhibition or work requires a knowledge of food values, the quantity to be supplied, and its preparation, exercise, watering, and many other factors, usually only acquired by years of experience.

Strict cleanliness of both the kennel and its occupants should always be the first consideration. No animal can be healthy if kept in a dirty state. The kennel floor should be cleaned daily and all excretions removed. Dogs are easily trained to be clean, and if they are exercised at regular hours they soon learn what is expected of them. As a kennel disinfectant a solution of permanganate of potash is recommended. This is obtainable at all chemists in crystal form and can be made up as required. It is far preferable to those disinfectants which emit a pungent odour or obnoxious emanations, and it completely oxidises putrefactive matter. Its only drawback is that it stains or discolours articles, though the discoloration gradually disappears.

When disease invades a kennel, particularly if it be of a contagious or infectious character, then the employment of a strong disinfectant is imperative. There are many such admirable preparations on the market.

Grooming, i.e., combing and brushing, is absolutely essential to prevent the hair matting, and for cleanliness, health, and glossy coats the brush applied externally once a day is a far better remedy than all the nostrums contained in the pharmacopœia. The dog, like the horse accustomed to grooming, will derive much benefit from the practice and look for it as regularly as he does his meals. Washing will depend to a great extent upon the work in which the dog is employed and upon the condition of the coat. If regularly groomed, a bath once a month is ample. A good bed of dry straw should be provided and it will be found that the dog will dry himself on this in his own fashion.

A proper system of feeding is one of the essentials of kennel management. In full work, two substantial meals per day are all that the Cocker Spaniel requires. *A meat ration is essential*, and it is one of the greatest fallacies to imagine that a dog can retain health and condition for any kind of work when deprived of meat for any length of time. The amount will vary according to the size of the dog, and the normally-sized Cocker (28 to 30 lb. in weight) should be fed raw meat at least three times each week; 6 oz. to 8 oz., cut up small and made appetising by the removal of surplus fat will provide that nourishment and stamina so necessary to successful breeding operations. Many breeders feed raw meat daily and believe 1 lb. at a meal is not excessive, but each animal must be treated for its individual requirements.

It is much the wiser plan to feed the bitch twice during the day; a meal equally proportioned night and morning will suffice to keep her fit and healthy, whereas with the dog his main meal should be given towards the evening-time. Never allow the young bitch to fast too long, and an occasional large meaty bone, avoiding the bones of rabbits, poultry, etc., which are apt to splinter and pierce the stomach, will be appreciated. Fresh green large bones are essential to good health in dogs, and should be given once or twice a week.

Green vegetables are of little value as a food for dogs, though a few chopped nettle tops mixed with broth provide a cooling medicine in the spring. Onion, spinach, and leeks cooked with a sheep's head add a piquancy and are of a certain amount of value as a laxative and for flavouring purposes, but cabbages and similar kinds of green vegetables should not be generally given. Finely-minced raw carrot added to the diet occasionally proves most beneficial. Potatoes are slow poison to many dogs and should be avoided when compiling the dietary scale. It is a wise plan to allow the kennel inmates free access to green fields, so that they may select the particular grass for which they display a penchant. Couch grass is specially favoured in this respect by most canines, and is taken apparently as a corrective medicine and not, as many people imagine, as indicating a desire for green vegetables.

CH. LOVABLE OF WARE
(Blue Roan)

Dogs should never be fed entirely on dry biscuits. Meat is generally obtainable, particularly if the kennel is situate in proximity to a town, at reasonable prices, and should be generously given. Though, in my opinion, biscuits should not form the staple diet, they allow the dog to make full use of his teeth and are a convenient food ready prepared and can be kept for lengthy periods without deterioration. Fatty meat is to be avoided, but if given it is preferable to do so in its raw state, that is, uncooked. When meat is cooked for broth or to provide gravy to mix with bread, biscuit, or meal, the fat should be skimmed off and discarded. Paunches or tripe are light and digestible, and given occasionally to puppies provide a welcome addition to the ordinary diet, but are not stamina-producing foods. Rice, wheat flour, maize meal, and oatmeal when well cooked may be given in small quantities and at infrequent intervals to provide a variation. Fish well boiled, and with the bones removed, when mixed with soaked bread or biscuit, provides a change, and the flesh of a kipper will frequently induce an appetite in a shy feeder. Eggs are easily digested, their food value is concentrated, and their use will be found invaluable for sick or ailing inmates of the kennel. One often hears milk condemned as a food for dogs as apt to induce worms, but it is the considered opinion of the writer when milk is given in small quantities, puppies thrive better than when it is withheld. It has been found that milk is best given alone and not with bread or other solids. Nevertheless, it should be remembered that fresh water should always be available and access thereto must never be denied on the grounds that milk has been supplied, for milk is a food and is not so satisfying to the dog for quenching its thirst as water.

To sum up, variation in diet is the keynote to successful feeding. Meat and concentrated foods are essential for growing stock, for all working dogs and brood bitches. The novice at first may easily fall into the error of over-feeding his dogs, and this must be guarded against. Sleek, flabby animals are good for neither work nor breeding purposes.

PUPPY REARING

For the first three weeks of their lives, puppies' requirements can usually be left to the dam, provided she is generously fed on nourishing foods given at frequent intervals, rather than in large meals. During the first week after whelping the nursing mother should be fed on milk foods, such as puddings, boiled fish in milk, etc., and an egg occasionally beaten up in milk will be found of benefit. At about four to five weeks the weaning process is generally started and this is brought to notice by the bitch vomiting some digested food for her puppies to eat, a hint from nature not to be misinterpreted. From now onwards any of the well-known milk food preparations should form the puppies' staple diet. There are many of these on the market, such as Lactol, Glaxo, Allenbury's and Benger's, all suitable, and the choice is merely a matter of personal opinion. Starting with two feeds a day of a dessertspoonful each, mixed in accordance with

Correct Shoulder Placement
and Front

Wrong narrow
Terrier front

the directions given, each puppy should be fed separately, for it will be found even at this early age that each one possesses an individuality of its own. Some are slower than others at feeding, others again are gluttons, whilst some will be found to be shy feeders and to need every encouragement. These peculiarities will soon become apparent to the keen observer, who will act accordingly. At six weeks three meals may be given per diem, and at about seven or eight weeks milk pudding in minute quantity may be added. From the sixth week a teaspoonful of carefully minced raw lean beef can be given, and from now onwards four meals should be provided each day. Once a week a ıaw fat breast of mutton given to the puppies to worry over is an excellent addition. If left to their own devices bitches in the wild state vomit food to their puppies, and this definitely should be borne in mind as indicative of nature's pointer that the puppies are requiring more than the bitch's milk and that solid food will do no harm. By this time the mother can be safely kept away from her puppies during the daytime and returned to the nest at night, more for the sake of the warmth she provides than for the supply of nourishment. In many cases a dam may be finally removed from the puppies when they are ten weeks old, when five to six meals, small in quantity and highly concentrated in character, should be given. Crusts from rusk bread soaked in gravy to which crumbs have been added, should be supplied, and the quantity of minced beef increased. Raw eggs and Glucose D or granulated sugar mixed with milk and bread crumbs are also an excellent diet. Spillers' Saval Puppy Food, or Spratt's Rodnim, may now be given in small quantities at one of the meals. In another fortnight the amount of food can be slightly increased and the number of meals reduced to four each day, and when the puppies are four months old these can be decreased to three. At six months of age the diet prescribed for the adult may be introduced, with the addition of large raw bones to which particles of meat still adhere. Backward puppies can be materially assisted by cod liver oil administered after meals —a teaspoonful each. Iodine has also of late been used with great success. Every opportunity should be given for exercise, and a mat, box, or small platform left in the sunniest corner of the run for the youngsters to curl up and sleep upon when tired of their gambols. Care must be taken never to over-fatigue young puppies; grave consequences frequently ensue from forcing the youngsters tc follow when on too long a walk. Their strength is over-taxed, although their spirit is willing; serious results, such as deformities, may accrue. Puppies should never be taken out on a collar and lead until at least six to seven months of age. Bad shoulders and bad fronts, so frequently seen, are in the main attributable to this reprehensible practice.

No artificial heating is required by Cocker Spaniels and such " coddling " methods produce hot-house plants, dogs incapable of performing their prescribed work in the field, devoid of stamina, and readily susceptible to chills and disease. Puppies should be treated for worms at four weeks and this should be done whether these pests indicate their presence or otherwise. Invariably every puppy harbours worms, and these must be eradicated if the youngster is to thrive. " Ruby " worm mixture has stood the test for years, is easily administered, safe, and efficacious. Another excellent worm medicine for puppies is Sherley's worm pills. The growth and development of puppies when in good health is gradual, but when a

Correct Thigh

cessation or lack of progress in growth is noticeable, the circumstance calls for an investigation and possibly an alteration in the dietary or environment. Cleanliness in the kennels is an absolute essential and should be inculcated at an early age.

The puppies may be kept together until about three months old; at this age many experienced breeders favour their being put out to " walk "—that is, a brace is placed with a farmer or cottager, where almost unfettered freedom

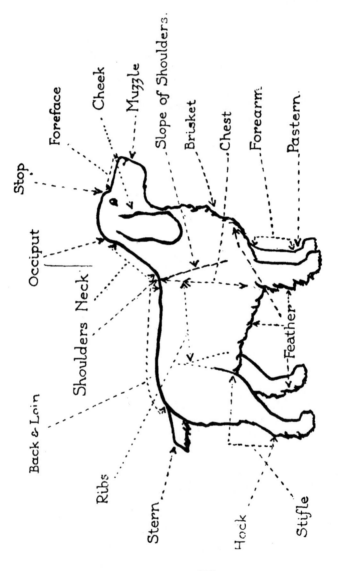

Stop
Foreface
Cheek
Muzzle
Slope of Shoulders.
Brisket
Chest
Forearm.
Pastern.
Occiput
Shoulders Neck
Back & Loin
Ribs
Stern
Hock
Stifle
Feather

E. K. W.
18.3.22.

DIAGRAM OF COCKER

108

is given. At nine months of age the puppies should be brought back to the kennel, and if intended for a show-bench schooling should commence.

PREPARING FOR EXHIBITION

It is now time for the puppy to become accustomed to the collar, but no attempt should be made as yet to attach a chain or lead. Merely encourage the youngster to follow when wearing the collar; this provides an opportunity to study his peculiarities and temperament, gain his trust and affection unreservedly, encourage him by kindness and remember that severity or reproof harshly administered may completely ruin a sensitive pupil.

After the lapse of a week, when the puppy has become accustomed to the collar, take him well away from the vicinity of the kennel to some open space which is new to him and attach the lead. If, without fighting the, to him, strange device, he follows, well and good, but do not tire him by prolonging the lesson; a few minutes will suffice during the first stages of tuition, then reward with some tit-bit and return to the kennel. On the other hand, should the pupil show fright at the lead or become fractious, jump around and is apparently in danger of strangling, carry him back to within a short distance of the kennel. When feeding time is approaching, liberate him with the lead still attached to the collar and allow him to drag the lead over the ground on his way back to participate in the good things going. He will be so intent in his hurried attempts to reach the food ere the other inmates have devoured his portion that he will overlook his dragging appendage. Repeat this lesson several times, and at the fourth or fifth attempt retain the lead in your hand and allow him to return to the kennel at his own pace. If this does not overcome his fright or antipathy to the lead, than a chain should be attached to his collar when the puppy is running loose at exercise. Care should be taken, however, that there are no protruding obstacles in which the chain might become fastened and our promising pupil's career thus come to an untimely end, perhaps, by hanging. When once the pupil follows on the lead he should be restrained from rushing forward and made to walk at heel at command. This is where firmness must be displayed by the handler, and it cannot

109

Photo]

CH. SILVER TEMPLA OF WARE
(Blue Roan)
Supreme Champion, Melbourne Royal Show, Australia.
Runner-up for the Supreme Championship of Cruft's 1937.

be too strongly emphasised that the one predominating factor in controlling dogs is FIRMNESS. Firmness—with kindness, not cruelty or coupled with undue severity, but firmness, first, last, and all the time.

By careful observation it will soon become apparent at what pace any dog looks at his best, and he should be encouraged to maintain that particular gait.

Muscular development can best be secured by what is termed " road work." This consists of regular exercise— and here, again, regularity must be strictly observed if the best results are desired—of long walks in country lanes, if possible, or across country. The pupil should be allowed to just strain at the lead until it is taut, for by this straining his muscles are brought into play to a far greater extent than when he is galloping aimlessly round.

THE COAT AND ITS CARE

To prepare the coat for exhibition the dog should be taken in hand several weeks before the event. A good washing is a first essential, and in this regard the writer has found Messrs. Cooper, McDougall & Robertson's " Sopex " an excellent preparation, also " Kur Mange," manufactured by the same firm, Sherley's Shampoo, etc., will be found an invaluable and preventive remedy for vermin. It may be mentioned here that no bitch during the œstrum period or in whelp should ever be washed or completely immersed in water. After the bath has been given to our prospective prize winner he should be given a thorough brushing and grooming on the day following. Next comes trimming, and here a word of warning is necessary to the novice, who is too prone to rely upon knives and scissors in this operation. Cutting the coat with these instruments is contrary to the regulations framed by the Kennel Club for preparing dogs for show, and if detected, which to a good judge is an easy matter, may entail disqualification both for the owner and dog. Frequently a dog may be turned out looking quite passable for the time being when trimmed with knife or scissors, but the disadvantage of the method will be brought home a few weeks later when the barbered coat has grown. It will look as if rats had been gnawing it. The correct way to trim is to carefully trim all the short body coat with a

No. 6 comb. This implement is obtainable at Messrs.
Spratts and other manufacturers of kennel accessories. For
the hair, or as it is technically termed, " the feathering,"
on the ears, legs, and under the body, a comb of larger
mesh should be used, and this sparingly, for it is desirable
to leave as much of these fringes on as is possible, for in
these days Cockers are, on the whole, not blessed with too
much feathering.

Take the No. 6 comb between the forefinger and the
thumb, holding the dog's skin firmly with the other
hand. A fair degree of pressure should be exerted in the
combing process and all the loose and dead hair combed

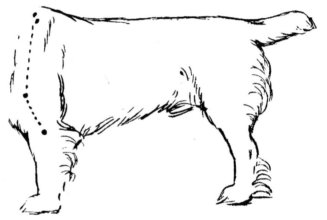

Wrong and upright shoulders, long back, and straight hocks

out. The top of the skull and ears should be treated in
the same manner, and it is particularly necessary to
remove all the " staring " hair from underneath the ears
and from the sides of the head, thus allowing the ears to
lie closer to the skull. The neck usually has an abundant
growth of hair, and this will require thinning, also the
outside of the legs, from where all old and discoloured
hair should be removed. Careful trimming of the legs
gives a neat appearance. The front of the chest, too,
requires to be carefully gone over and much of the frill
can be removed by the finger and thumb, a method
usefully to be employed in trimming the stray locks on

ears, shoulders and hocks. It will be found a far easier task for one person to hold the dog in an upright position and for an assistant to manipulate the comb. It will be necessary to cut out any matted hair between the toes and under the feet.

A course of linseed oil, a dessertspoonful given in the food or separately after meals, for ten days prior to starting to trim will render the hair more amenable and will add lustre to the coat. If the animal is very rough in coat, a preparation of equal parts of neat's-foot oil and paraffin, well mixed with flowers of sulphur, should be rubbed into the coat a week before the bath is given. The operation is a tiring one both for the subject and the manipulator, but it is advisable to complete the process at one sitting. After trimming, the dog should be well groomed with a hound glove and finished off with a chamois leather or hand massage, whilst on the following day the dog should be gone over carefully to see that stray hairs have not stuck up out of their place.

Never wash the dog less than a week before the show. Most of the natural grease is removed from the skin by washing, which loosens the scurf and this takes a few days to be brushed out. By washing fully a week before the show it gives the skin the opportunity to exhale natural grease, and this will give the glossy and sleek appearance so desirable. Rinsing in graded temperature water, reducing down almost to blood heat, is advised, and a little glycerine in the last rinse is advised. During the process of trimming the dog should be released and allowed to scamper around the road or enclosure. This will afford him an opportunity of stretching himself and accord him a welcome relief from a cramped and constrained position. He should be carefully observed during these intervals to note the progress made and what other parts still require trimming, otherwise too much or too little may have been removed, and the time will be well spent in watching the progress.

During the whole course of preparing for show the dog should be generously fed on a meat diet, and regularly exercised. Taken out on a lead, he should be made to stand still at intervals, " posing " him in his most attractive position, with ears and tail down and head erect. After a few lessons he will soon learn what is required, and

I 113

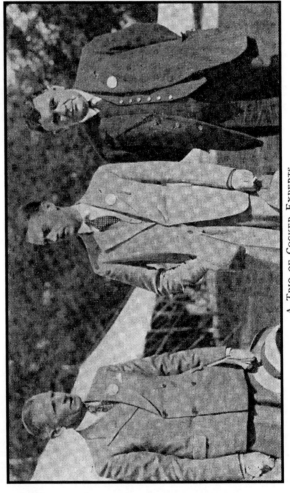

A Trio of Cocker Experts

Left to right: Capt. J. McTaggart, Mons. C. Daniel Lacombe, and Mr. H. T. Davis

114

will assume this posed attitude in a natural manner when stopped in his walk. It must be remembered that a dog with correct deportment and gait readily attracts the judge's attention when in the ring. Encourage him to allow strangers to handle him, also accustom him to the close proximity of other dogs on leads. Rewarding when he displays to your satisfaction, and withholding the tit-bit when he does otherwise, will soon teach him the lessons of what is generally termed " ring craft." When actually in the ring, a point for the novice to remember is, never to draw the judge's attention to a fault possessed by the dog through constantly looking

Apple head, pinched face, and high set on of ears

at that fault. Frequently the beginner gives himself away in his endeavours to hide a particular failing by unconsciously attracting the judge's attention to it by apprehensive glances.

Another point to remember is to devote your entire attention to your own exhibit. The dog will not be slow to take advantage of any relaxing of vigilance; he will possibly endeavour to enter into canine conversation with his nearest competitor, or even lie down in the ring at the moment the judge is summing up his good qualities. It is always advisable to convey the dog to the show in a hamper or box. The vagaries of the weather are thus

Group—Cocker Club Championship Show, 1933

in a great measure combated and the animal arrives fresh and without that buffeting about to which he might be subjected if accompanying his master in a crowded train.

On reaching the show and when the veterinary examination is over, lose no time in placing the dog on his allotted bench, where he should be allowed to rest. Offer him a drink of water, but if he does not wish to quench his thirst, remove the dish at once, in order that he has no opportunity to dip his ears or feet into the water and thus mar his appearance. A little food may be given, followed by a sharp walk round the show yard to enable him to relieve himself. Then back to the bench and the final grooming, until warned by the steward that the class is about to be judged. Don't trail him about all over the show, as there is nothing so tiring for the animal as this aimless wandering around while his master indulges in conversation with all and sundry. He may get trodden upon or kicked, thus be lamed at the crucial moment. He should come into the ring feeling refreshed and moving brightly and merrily. When the judging is over, return him to his bench, removing him at intervals of a few minutes each during the day to attend to nature's wants and for a little exercise. Remember, your dog is an exhibition, and if every exhibitor removed his dog from the benches all the day it would be unfair to the public who have paid to see the exhibits.

Always remember that a good loser makes a good winner, and that an exhibitor who cannot meet " triumph and disaster " in an equable spirit will not go far in the game. Never criticise the judge's awards—those who overhear you will think of you as a disappointed exhibitor. Far better to take the decision in silence, however unjust it may seem, then when the judging is over, ask the judge to kindly go over your dog and tell you what, in his opinion, are its good or bad points. Tell the judge that you are merely a beginner and you will find that he will be only too willing to explain his reason for his awards.

A good dog will always come to the front. If it does not receive its due reward on the first few occasions shown, do not be discouraged; the day will surely come when you will lead it from the ring with the coveted red ticket in your hand. Judges, like all humans, have their little failings and fancies. Some prefer one type of dog and others the direct opposite. What may be considered a grave fault by one judge will be passed over with a lenient eye by another. The name of the judge is always given in the show schedule, and if you know that he is a faddist on any particular point on which your dog fails, then do not enter under him. It is far better not to exhibit than to show and then grouse. Never commit the unpardonable offence of arguing with the judge or insisting that your dog has been badly treated.

With Cocker Spaniels, many faults are hidden from the unskilled eye by coat and feathering. The same dog when shown with a profusion of body feather and ear fringe will look a very different animal when out of coat, the latter a circumstance frequently the cause of a reversal in the awards, and to the novice a procedure sometimes difficult to understand. He must remember that the condition of the animal, or, as the club standard puts it, " general appearance," due to lack of coat, detracts from the general contour and warrants a judge in reversing a previous favourable decision. This condition of coat, health, thinness or fatness, all help to make or mar and are taken into consideration by the judge when making his awards.

A very sound piece of advice to all exhibitors is to concentrate attention entirely upon the dog whilst in the ring and not to allow your mind or that of your dog's to wander. Take the matter seriously and the dog will do likewise and rise to his best for the occasion.

CHAPTER IV

But if the shady woods my cares employ
In quest of feathered game, my Spaniels beat,
Puzzling th' entangled copse; and from the brake
Push forth the whirring pheasant; high in air
He waves his varied plumes, stretching away
With hasty wing, Soon, from th' unlifted tube
The mimic thunder bursts, the leaden death
O'ertakes him; and, with many a giddy whirl,
To earth he falls, and at my feet expires.

Somerville.

BREEDING PRINCIPLES

FUNDAMENTAL Principles of Breeding Live Stock
—Characteristics of Strain—Experiments—Mating
Champion Dog and Champion Bitch—Transmitting
Faults—Soundness—Tail Placement—Size in the Brood
Bitch—"Type"—Fashion in Cockers—In-breeding—
Line Breeding—Best Age for Stud Dog to Sire Puppies
—Undermining the Constitution—Breeding Table—
Rosslyn Bruce on Stud Force—The Bitch's First Season
—The Stud Dog—Conditions for Service—Colour Breed-
ing—Self-coloured and Parti-coloured—Difficulty of
Perpetuating Reds—The Descriptive Standard of the
Cocker Spaniel as adopted by the Cocker Spaniel Club—
The Scale of Points for Judging Cocker Spaniels.

ASSUMING the novice to be in ignorance of the fundamental principles of breeding live stock, he is advised at the outset to carefully study the pedigrees of the many outstanding dogs of the variety. The reasons for this will disclose themselves later.

When the foundation of the kennel has been established by the purchase of one or more brood bitches, and the novice has in mind the ideal or type he aims at, the next question to arise is the production from his own kennel of progeny conforming nearer to the ideal than the parents. In a nutshell, this is the whole object of breeding, for without such an ideal breeding is merely a waste of energy, time, and money. It is here that a knowledge of the strains as given in Chapter II will be found of assistance. To mate a dog and bitch without a definite object

119

in view is not scientific breeding. The good and bad points and those of their immediate forebears should be carefully studied. It is wrong to breed from an immature bitch, because this arrests the growth, and the same is applicable to the stud dog—the puppies lack vigour and stamina.

Pedigrees should be examined, not from the angle of so many names, but each should convey to the breeder the type of the individual dog it represents. An excellent plan before mating a bitch is to set out her pedigree and that of the stud dog selected for at least five generations. Under each name insert the faults or good points which the owner of the name is known to have possessed. If it is found that on both sides any particular fault or faults is strongly predominant, then the union of the descendants is likely to reproduce the fault in a greater degree.

Example:—

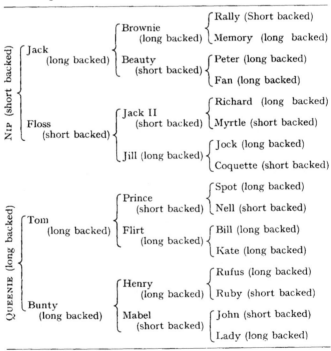

It will be noticed that the preponderancy both in the proposed sire and dam tends towards an excessive length of back, hence, another stud dog whose faults in this respect are less prominent should be selected. Avoid going to extremes in all breeding matters, as a dog excelling individually in one characteristic (as apart from " family " influence) but rarely stamps his progeny with the same outstanding characteristic.

It should always be remembered that the stud dog may not be a true representative of the family to which he

F.T. CH. JAZZ OF FEWS
Field Trial Champion.

belongs, and it is quite probable that certain characteristics of his strain, which he does not display, may be apparent in his offspring. Other characteristics foreign to the family or strain, and which he possesses, may not be transmitted to the progeny; hence the importance of ascertaining the good and bad points of his parents " even unto the fifth generation."

A fact well known to breeders is that certain families never cross well with others, and as it is important that the blood of the dog should suit, or " nick with," as it is termed, the bitch, it will be again seen how a careful study of the pedigrees of the different outstanding specimens of the breed will repay the time expended on their perusal.

Experiments in breeding should never be attempted by the novice, even if he has preconceived ideas of the ideal at which to aim. Time may be well spent in writing for stud cards or pedigrees of what are generally recognised as the best dogs of the day. These should be carefully studied and a knowledge acquired of the various strains, which when mated together have produced our modern champions. Armed with this knowledge, the novice is in

Photo]   CH. BENET OF WARE   [Fall
The only Orange and White Champion

a better position to acquire a brood bitch of the type and owning the qualities desired.

An old adage, and one as true to-day as when first uttered, is that " Like begets like." However, this can be, and is, frequently misinterpreted. For instance, the mating of a champion dog with a champion bitch will most likely result in nondescript progeny, *unless* the blood lines or family of both are more or less similar. Should the sire's family show a tendency to ultra-short backs and the family of the dam are predisposed to long backs, the results of the union cannot be expected to follow the middle course and assume backs of the desired length. They are much more likely some to take after the sire, others after the dam, and thus the faults of both are perpetuated.

Faults are more easily transmitted than are the good qualities. Assuming that a particular dog, good in all essentials except that he possesses an undershot mouth, is mated back to his own family strain with a view to " fixing " his own good qualities, the result will be in all probability to fix the undesirable characteristic. Defects are only to be equalised and improved if only existing in one of the parents and totally absent in the other. It is far better to use as a sire a moderately good specimen possessing no outstanding faults and of no salient merit; mated to a bitch of similar character—one whose family is known to possess no essential differences to that of the sire, the results may reach the highest degree of perfection. It would be an error to imagine that by mating a small-sized bitch to a large stud dog the union would produce a litter of puppies which will all become good-sized dogs. More often than not, the result would be that some of the litter would have a large head on a small body; others a small head on a large body; others again would be leggy with a short body, and some would probably own a powerful body supported by short legs. A study of the history of the Cocker Spaniel proves that with a few exceptions " family " plays a far greater part in producing the desired type than do individual dogs. Mating a dog and bitch without a fixed plan, i.e., without cognisance of the characteristics of their respective families, is not scientific breeding. The points to be considered are: (1) families, (2) blood relationship, (3) age, (4) appearance, (5) capabilities and character. Too much importance cannot be attached to the characteristics required in the breed, robustness of constitution, good heart room, spring of rib, depth of brisket and powerful quarters, coupled with plenty of substance, far outweigh the finer points, such as texture of ear feathering, length of muzzle, or shade of eye. A Cocker Spaniel lacking the character and vivacity of the breed, which the spring of rib and power behind do so much to assist, can never be typical. Soundness in constitution, soundness in movement fore and aft, and last, but by no means least, soundness in intellect, are essentials in perpetuating healthy stock. Referring to

TABLE SHOWING WHEN A BITCH IS DUE TO WHELP

Served January	Due to Whelp March	Served February	Due to Whelp April	Served March	Due to Whelp May	Served April	Due to Whelp June	Served May	Due to Whelp July	Served June	Due to Whelp August	Served July	Due to Whelp September	Served August	Due to Whelp October	Served September	Due to Whelp November	Served October	Due to Whelp December	Served November	Due to Whelp January	Served December	Due to Whelp February
1	5	1	5	1	3	1	3	1	3	1	3	1	2	1	3	1	3	1	3	1	3	1	2
2	6	2	6	2	4	2	4	2	4	2	4	2	3	2	4	2	4	2	4	2	4	2	3
3	7	3	7	3	5	3	5	3	5	3	5	3	4	3	5	3	5	3	5	3	5	3	4
4	8	4	8	4	6	4	6	4	6	4	6	4	5	4	6	4	6	4	6	4	6	4	5
5	9	5	9	5	7	5	7	5	7	5	7	5	6	5	7	5	7	5	7	5	7	5	6
6	10	6	10	6	8	6	8	6	8	6	8	6	7	6	8	6	8	6	8	6	8	6	7
7	11	7	11	7	9	7	9	7	9	7	9	7	8	7	9	7	9	7	9	7	9	7	8
8	12	8	12	8	10	8	10	8	10	8	10	8	9	8	10	8	10	8	10	8	10	8	9
9	13	9	13	9	11	9	11	9	11	9	11	9	10	9	11	9	11	9	11	9	11	9	10
10	14	10	14	10	12	10	12	10	12	10	12	10	11	10	12	10	12	10	12	10	12	10	11
11	15	11	15	11	13	11	13	11	13	11	13	11	12	11	13	11	13	11	13	11	13	11	12
12	16	12	16	12	14	12	14	12	14	12	14	12	13	12	14	12	14	12	14	12	14	12	13
13	17	13	17	13	15	13	15	13	15	13	15	13	14	13	15	13	15	13	15	13	15	13	14
14	18	14	18	14	16	14	16	14	16	14	16	14	15	14	16	14	16	14	16	14	16	14	15
15	19	15	19	15	17	15	17	15	17	15	17	15	16	15	17	15	17	15	17	15	17	15	16
16	20	16	20	16	18	16	18	16	18	16	18	16	17	16	18	16	18	16	18	16	18	16	17
17	21	17	21	17	19	17	19	17	19	17	19	17	18	17	19	17	19	17	19	17	19	17	18
18	22	18	22	18	20	18	20	18	20	18	20	18	19	18	20	18	20	18	20	18	20	18	19
19	23	19	23	19	21	19	21	19	21	19	21	19	20	19	21	19	21	19	21	19	21	19	20
20	24	20	24	20	22	20	22	20	22	20	22	20	21	20	22	20	22	20	22	20	22	20	21
21	25	21	25	21	23	21	23	21	23	21	23	21	22	21	23	21	23	21	23	21	23	21	22
22	26	22	26	22	24	22	24	22	24	22	24	22	23	22	24	22	24	22	24	22	24	22	23
23	27	23	27	23	25	23	25	23	25	23	25	23	24	23	25	23	25	23	25	23	25	23	24
24	28	24	28	24	26	24	26	24	26	24	26	24	25	24	26	24	26	24	26	24	26	24	25
25	29	25	29	25	27	25	27	25	27	25	27	25	26	25	27	25	27	25	27	25	27	25	26
26	30	26	30	26	28	26	28	26	28	26	28	26	27	26	28	26	28	26	28	26	28	26	27
27	31	27	1 (MAY)	27	29	27	29	27	29	27	29	27	28	27	29	27	29	27	29	27	29	27	28
28	1 (APR)	28	2	28	30	28	30	28	30	28	30	28	29	28	30	28	30	28	30	28	30	28	1 (MAR)
29	2	29	3	29	31	29	1 (JULY)	29	31	29	31	29	30	29	31	29	31	29	31	29	31	29	2
30	3			30	1 (JUNE)	30	2	30	1 (AUG)	30	1 (SEP)	30	1 (OCT)	30	1 (NOV)	30	2 (DEC)	30	1	30	1 (JAN)	30	3 (FEB)
31	4			31	2			31	2			31	2	31	2			31	2			31	4

the chapter on strains, it will be noted that practically the whole breed is derived from a few strains, and that when these strains were properly combined, fixity of type was achieved and typical specimens resulted. Several strains transmit peculiarities or eccentricities. One strain, in particular, shows peculiar gait behind, and it rarely happens that this peculiarity can be bred out in less than two generations. The Cocker's hind action should invariably demonstrate his cheerful nature. All of his body should be constantly moving when in action; the wriggle

ROBINHURST OF WARE
(Red, American Bred)

of the hindquarters and continuous tail movement is an essential. In this latter respect the placement of the tail below the level of the back is indispensable. In exactly the same manner as a terrier loses its terrier-like character and fire by a low-set tail, the whole characteristic of a Cocker is lacking if its tail is high set-on and carried at too gay an angle. The difference is discernible to the veriest tyro, and the great advantage in the matter of '' finish '' given by correct tail placement and carriage is readily apparent.

When selecting a brood bitch, strive to hit the happy medium in size. Do not be persuaded by that stock phrase: " The bitch can do with more length of back to advantage." This is a common but erroneous belief, and one disproved from actual experience. A brood bitch of moderate quality all through, with no glaring faults, combining soundness with average size, should be chosen. When such a bitch mated to a given sire is found to reproduce her own type, it is a wise plan to continue to mate her to that dog. When selecting a mate for such a bitch, particular attention should be given to the maternal side of both sire and dam. English breeders are giving more attention to the " Bruce Lowe " system, which consists, briefly, in the theory that the best qualities are transmitted through the female line, and a stud dog bred from a superlative bitch coming from a good " family " and showing those family characteristics to a marked degree is the dog to use.

Certain dogs possess the knack of stamping their progeny with their best features and a study of their pedigree will usually show that the dam is responsible for this; a " chance got " good looking dog rarely reproduces himself. The valuable influence to the breed of certain stud dogs possessing great hereditary power may be principally observed in the female progeny, though occasionally the law of inheritance results in a crosswise transmission; that is, the female progeny show the qualities of the sire and the male offspring the characteristics of the dam. Puppies sired by a moderately good dog out of a superlative bitch whose dam also was of the same quality, are far more likely to produce good stock than the progeny of a moderate bitch when mated to a superlative dog. Keep as near to the standard (see pages 147-149) as possible, and do not allow variations in the matter of size to weigh too heavily. Size is not such a great fault as bad architecture. If the animal in question is correct in type and character, better results will be obtained by utilising such a one for breeding purposes, than another, possibly ideal in size, yet not possessing what, for the lack of a better term, is called " type."

Fashion decrees various changes from time to time, but these are usually short-lived, and in all material respects type has remained very little changed during the past twenty years. From time to time, fashions or crazes have tended to exalt one particular good point above its true value. These fashions are generally attributable to the influence or popularity of some particular stud or show dog possessing that point in a marked degree. If these crazes were permitted without restraint or check, we should soon see that particular part or point overshadowing the whole, and in a few generations the breed would be changed beyond recognition. It is the standard of points as laid down by the club that serves the valuable purpose of restraining these fashions or crazes. Hence, I would again emphasise the importance of keeping as close to the standard as possible.

The knowledge gained by a careful comparison of the pedigrees of outstanding dogs should enable the beginner to determine the strain to " nick in " with his own stock and in such a measure as to strengthen the points most desired.

A perusal of the pedigrees and family lines of the Cocker Spaniel go to show that in-breeding has been extensively practised. Doubtless, in the past—for various and good reasons—this was unavoidable. To it is attributable the evolution of a fixed type, but in-breeding cannot be carried on indefinitely. All varieties of dogs were produced originally from accidental or local variations in the prototype. These variations were accentuated and preserved by selective in-breeding of specimens which showed the variations in the most marked manner. Thus it will readily be seen that all pedigree stock is to some extent in-bred.

The following extract is well worth every breeder's careful consideration:—

> " Coming by chance upon a 'Stud force', which had proved himself easily the best of his breed in the production of progeny of a particular type in a species not so very far removed from Terriers, the Factor ventured a little gamble that it would be found that he was in-bred; on inquiry it proved that two sisters were mated to their own sire, and a daughter mated to a son of the other, a female from this mating was put to the original sire, and the resulting daughter mated to a male, whose sire and dam were both by the original male.

A Group of Famous "of Ware" Cocker Spaniels

Every one is a Challenge Certificate winner. Collectively they have won upwards of 150 Certificates. *Back row*: Silver Flare, Lucky Star, Gay Knight, Silver Sonnet, Diana. *Front row*: Whoopee, Silver Templa, Otto, Benet, and Sovereign. Owner, the Author, Mr. H. S. Lloyd.

It is the result of this intensely in-bred cross which is to-day the supreme sire of his species. The strong constitution, which was a feature of the original male, has been fully established, and even, if possible, enhanced. You can in-breed to constitutional strength, just as you can in-breed to constitutional weakness in all mammals; this fact is often overlooked."

Rosslyn Bruce, *Our Dogs*, 13/5/32.

Now that the breed is well established, line breeding has been found to be far more satisfactory. Briefly, the principle of line breeding is the selection of a specimen descended from a line or family, possessing the desired characteristic. Line breeding can be carried on for years without recourse to a vast amount of in-breeding. Once a female line is established that can be relied upon to reproduce itself more than half the battle is won, and if care is taken to select sires whose " family " or blood is in no way antagonistic, most of the breeder's problems will solve themselves.

The exact degree which each or both the parents contribute to the progeny cannot be determined, but it is a remarkable fact that when desirable qualities have been secured, such are nearly always accompanied by an undesirable one. Thus, in Fox Terriers, breeders who aimed for long heads achieved the desideratum, but found their long-headed dogs were too long-bodied. A somewhat similar occurrence holds good in Cocker Spaniel breeding —short backs and short neck go together. In order to produce a longer neck, selective breeding was resorted to and large-sized dogs and bitches utilised. Consequent upon this an outcry was raised to the effect that the breed was being ruined, that the Cocker Spaniel was being bred too large, and that his identity as a separate variety would soon be lost and merged in the Springer or Field Spaniel. Thoughtful breeders, however, had only used these large specimens as a means to an end. The question of size automatically adjusted itself after a generation or so when once the desired longer neck had been secured. To-day, necks combined with short backs are all that could be desired in the coloured Cocker Spaniel, though in the blacks there is still a slight tendency to shorter necks, and this is doubtless attributable to the fact that originally the blacks were longer in back. It will take a few generations to achieve the desired combination. Even at the time of writing a marked improvement is apparent.

It is a popular belief that a stud dog sires his best puppies when from two to four years of age. My personal experience leads me to believe that within reasonable limits the question of age is not so important as many imagine. I consider that soundness of constitution, together with the suitability of blood lines to those of the bitch, are the chief factors.

BLACK FRIAR OF WARE
(Black)

Provided that their constitutions have not been undermined by too early or continuous breeding, I have found that the average Cocker Spaniel bitch produces her best litters when aged between two to four years. It is true, though, that cases are on record of quite aged bitches rearing offspring of outstanding merit, but here again, in my opinion, these exceptions prove the rule.

When a certain stud dog has been decided upon, it is advisable to book a service to him forthwith, and at the same time inform his owner of the approximate period the bitch is due to require service.

The novice, in order to avoid disappointment and possible loss, should clearly understand the customs for service arrangements. The stud fee or the amount charged for the service carries no guarantee that puppies will result from the mating; in other words, the fee paid is for the service only. It behoves the owner of the bitch, therefore, to select as a sire a dog which has a proven record as such. The services of popular sires are in great demand, hence the necessity for early booking. In the event of a litter not resulting, the return of the stud fee is not legally enforceable, though in actual practice most owners of stud dogs interpret the terms in the widest and most generous spirit, allowing a second service where the bitch has failed to produce puppies. This second service, as will be gathered from the preceding remarks, is likewise not legally enforceable—it is an act of courtesy —and the owner of the stud dog is within his rights, as defined by custom, in insisting that the second service be to the same bitch and at her next ensuing season or œstrum.

The payer of the stud fee has the right to be present in order to satisfy himself that the service has been efficiently carried out and by the dog to which he has booked. Custom lays it down that the owner of a stud dog (which has not given proof of siring progeny) should notify that fact, unless it is definitely understood between the parties that the service is in the nature of a trial to " prove " the siring qualities of the stud dog. It is advisable to have all such arrangements set out in writing, and in case (as is sometimes arranged) the owner of the stud dog agrees to take first or second choice of the prospective litter in lieu of a stud fee, this agreement also should be in writing, but in the long run the novice owner will find it cheaper to pay the stud fees usually asked and obtained.

A bitch usually comes into season about every six months, when it will be observed that there is some change of manner. The first indication is an enlargement of the genital organs, followed by a discharge of blood lasting from eight to ten days. The right time for mating is when the blood (" colour ") turns white, which varies from

131

the ninth to the twelfth day. Some bitches will stand at the fourth day, whilst some not until the thirteenth day. The best time for mating is the eleventh day and not later, as very often after this time it has been found that conception has not resulted. Even earlier, say the ninth day, if a service can be obtained, may be quite successful, as the sperm of the male lives for nearly fourteen days. It should, however, be borne in mind that Nature does not react to any simple rule of thumb calculation and that every bitch is an individual and should be treated as such.

DAME FORTUNE OF WARE
(Black and White Ticked)

The reason that a bitch does not conceive is often because her vaginal discharge reacts acid and kills the sperm; in such a case it is only necessary to neutralise this acid discharge, if this is discovered to be the trouble. Very rarely can a case of non-breeding be attributed to the faults of sterility or impotence in the dog. A course of " Wheat Germ " Oil is advised if a bitch fails to reproduce after several attempts. During service, the bitch should be kept on a short lead and prevented from sitting down. In the majority of cases all will go well, but sometimes the service has to be forced. In such troublesome cases the bitch should be muzzled and kept on a short lead whilst a second person takes hold of her and thrusts an arm between the hind legs to prevent her sitting or moving about. During the perfectly normal procedure of copulation (the tie), which may last from ten minutes to one hour, care must be taken that the bitch does not try to sit down or an injury to the stud dog may result. After service the bitch should rest for a short time before being taken home, and the dog should be walked about for a few minutes. One visit is enough. Many breeders prefer two services in the case of young or of old and fat bitches. If

two services are agreed upon, the second should take place within 24 hours. Whether conception has resulted or not can only be detected after the lapse of four or five weeks; in some cases even later.

The period of normal gestation is 63 days, but in the majority of cases the time is 60, 61, 62, or even 59 days. It is important that the novice should pay special attention to the bitch when she shows the first signs of being in

GALTREES RAVEN

season, and a note should be made of the date, otherwise disappointments may ensue. Very often breeders send their bitches to the stud dog on the fifth day, or perhaps the fourteenth day, thinking it was the ninth, tenth, or eleventh day; in such cases a bitch has often to be returned unmated because she was too early or too late in season, thus necessitating another visit.

One of the first indications of conception is that the bitch eats indifferently, or she may vomit her food, or whine when lying down. At the expiration of about five weeks one can generally observe a rounding of the flanks, and the nipples become slightly enlarged. As the filling of the flanks proceeds in the latter stages of pregnancy, say, from the sixth week onwards, the bitch should be fed three times daily instead of the usual one big meal. The expansion of the matrix produces a continuous pressure upon the digestive organs, hence the need for more frequent feeding.

It is necessary to well feed the expectant mother with milk, meat and bones, and nutritives such as are contained in Virol, Cod Liver Oil, Oxo, eggs, etc., which should be added freely to assist bone-making, but phosphates of lime should be avoided. She should be daily exercised in the open air, and care taken that no violent exertion such as jumping be indulged in within eight or ten days of whelping.

It is important to free the bitch from worms eight days before mating, and again a fortnight after service. Eight days before whelping cleanse the breast with a good antiseptic wash and afterwards wash the same part daily with soap and water. This should destroy the " hairlings " (parasites) which otherwise probably would be conveyed to the puppies when feeding. *More puppies are lost from worms than from distemper.*

Whelping usually takes place at night or early in the morning. The interval between the birth of each puppy is generally from half-an-hour to one hour; sometimes longer. Should any complications arise, the novice will be well advised to call in a good veterinary surgeon without delay, and meanwhile apply hot compresses to the abdomen, or try soft, gentle massage. For whelping, use the special type of box which has been found excellent for the purpose. Its dimensions are about 2 ft. by 2 ft. by

Ch. Irrepressible of Ware
(Blue Roan)

136

2 ft. high; the top can be opened like a box, and the front is likewise hinged and let down. Around the sides is a 4-in. board, like a shelf, five inches from the floor. This shelf or ledge prevents the mother from laying on and suffocating or crushing a puppy against the side of the box—a not uncommon occurrence with a large litter. On the floor of the box lay a clean disinfected sack, and when the puppies are two days old this should be replaced with soft, sun-dried hay. Later, straw can be used. The bitch should not be troubled by the presence of strangers whilst whelping; neither should she be excited, but left alone as much as possible.

During the first 24 hours after whelping, no solid food should be given to the mother, but milk foods such as Benger's, Allenbury's, Lactol, groats, or other similar easily digested milk products with plenty of sugar added may be given freely, followed in about 48 hours with sheep's head broth, etc. In the early days her milk may not be plentiful enough, especially with a bitch at her first whelping, and in order to help the formation of milk, give boiled linseed with the food, adding the water to the linseed. The puppies should be examined as to constitutional or physical defects, and any malformed ones should be destroyed at once. It is very important not to allow even the strongest mother to nurse more than five or six puppies. One can often tell from the size of the bitch if she is going to have a large litter and thus bespeak the services of a suitable foster-mother due to whelp at the same time. The whelping of the bitch and foster-mother should as nearly as possible synchronise, as the composition of the milk is continuously changing, becoming richer in quality as time goes on. Sometimes there will be a little trouble to persuade the foster-mother to take the puppies, but it can generally be overcome in the following manner. The foster is temporarily removed, and during her absence the puppies are introduced into her nest and rubbed against the foster's own offspring to acquire her scent. On her return she finds only the strangers, and if she allows them to feed and cleans them, then all is well. If no foster is obtainable, it is a matter of consideration as to whether the puppies in excess of five in number should be destroyed. It is practically useless to try and rear them on the bottle; the result rarely justifies the enormous and constant trouble entailed. In selecting the puppies to be destroyed, select the weaker ones, which feel softer to the touch. The harder and heavier ones leave with the mother.

If dew claws are present, remove them on the third or fourth day with a pair of rounded operating scissors, previously sterilising with iodine. About the same time,

Photo]   WANDA OF WOODHAW   [Hedges, Lytham
(Blue Roan)
The Certificate winner at Cruft's, 1935.

the puppies' tails should be shortened by removing a trifle over half with a pair of scharp scissors, previously sterilised. These operations are very simple, and the cleansing and healing can be left to the mother's care; in three days the cuts should heal.

For the first three weeks leave the feeding of the puppies to the mother, taking good care that she herself is well fed three times daily, and that after the first week she is given plenty of exercise in the open; the bedding should be changed frequently and everything possible done to discourage and destroy flies.

About the third week the teeth pierce through the gums, indicating that the puppies can be fed with fine-cut or scraped beef, starting with very small quantities —a teaspoonful for each puppy. Care and attention to the feeding of puppies is vital to their future welfare; whatever is neglected in the first six weeks can never be remedied later. The rearing of puppies is an art which only experience can teach, and it is said that " the bringer-up of a puppy can do as much good or as much harm as the breeder." A well-bred puppy in bad hands has very little chance of becoming a fine specimen, whilst a medium quality one in experienced hands will improve wonderfully. It is not the breeder alone who is responsible for the ultimate quality of the puppies, but the keeper (or rearer) has an important share.

A bitch should never be bred from at her first season, but exceptions have been, and may be, made in the case of a young bitch whose season comes on in the early spring. The hard and fast rule should be made, however, never to breed from a maiden bitch should her first season be in winter. It is also inadvisable to allow a bitch to go past her third year without breeding from her. Again, a bitch should not be bred each time she comes in season. One litter a year is the maximum, otherwise stamina and powers of resistance to disease will be reduced and the puppies will be weakly constituted, and if they do not die young will become victims of disease or grow into weedy specimens lacking bone and substance. But, where there are good reasons for more frequent breeding to be resorted to and a bitch has reared two successive litters, she should invariably be given a rest during the winter months.

A method frequently adopted with success is to " collect up " the blood of an outstanding specimen. By this is meant the utilisation of blood relations with a view to the production of an individual dog possessing the same characteristics as the model. Further, by this process these characteristics will become established and fixed, as also, it should be carefully noted, will the faults. For instance, we will assume that a dog known as A is a model of his breed as near the ideal as possible, and in order to collect up his blood we will proceed somewhat as follows. His pedigree reads:—

Sire—A	{	C {	G H
		D {	L F
Dam—B	{	E {	A M
		Q {	A Y

The result of mating A and B would be a treble cross of A, thus intensifying the characteristics of A in its own progeny. This system is capable of many variations, and provided it is utilised in moderation is safe, but care should be taken on each and every occasion that the stamina and constitution of each dog mated is beyond criticism.

Briefly, the value of a study of pedigrees in dog breeding lies in its utilisation for transmitting family attributes to the progeny of any chosen union. It is noteworthy that the influence of near ancestors is more strongly reproduced in the progeny than those more remote, so that individual excellence on *both* sides of the family tree, rather than the length of or number of names it contains, should be the breeder's aim. In other words, '' pedigree '' is neither more nor less than careful selection.

COLOUR BREEDING

Little is known of the chemistry of pigmentation, and this subject presents an almost virgin field for research and investigation. Nevertheless, to the experienced breeder it is a most fascinating study. Cocker Spaniels are, at the present time, divided into three sections, namely: Reds or Goldens, Blacks, and Other Than Blacks, Reds or Goldens. The day is not far distant when the categories will be increased, as it is in America, where the breed is divided into Self coloured and Parti-coloured. Self coloured include blacks, livers, and reds, while Parti-coloureds embrace all other colours, including blue roans, liver roans, lemon roans, red roans, black and white, liver and white, lemon and white, tri-colour black and tans and liver and liver and tans—the two last-mentioned, it is interesting to

MERRYBROOK OF CRAVEN
(Blue Roan, New Zealand)

note, are frequently the product of self-coloured parents. Therefore, after a careful survey of the particulars appearing in a pedigree, it should be a simple matter to keep self colours and parti-colours entirely separate, if such is the object; though when it is desired to perpetuate some particular characteristic it may be found desirable to mate self-coloured with parti-coloured. When mating two blue roans the result is generally parti-coloured puppies, and it does not necessarily follow that the litter will take after their parents in colouring; frequently they will be black

141

and white, lemon and white, or even liver and white. More often than not a preponderance of blue roans can be relied upon from such a mating, with an occasional black and white puppy in the litter. From my own experience and that of other breeders with whom I have discussed this subject, it would appear that a black and white puppy from such a union when mated to a blue roan will in turn invariably produce blue roans.

INTERNATIONAL CH. WILFUL WISTARIA
(France)

A writer in *Country Life* of 20/1/1900 gives a most interesting discourse which may prove of the utmost interest to those who delve deeply into the colour question:—

"The question of colour is, I believe, vastly more important to breeders than is generally believed. I think it is an indication of breed. The

142

late Mr. Laverack thought so, too, and believed that a cross between a brother and sister, the one lemon and white, and the other black and white or 'Blue', as he called the ticked dogs, was as good as an outside cross for perpetuating the vitality of the race. . . .

"The one thing common to him and all breeders of domestic animals was that of trying to breed from near relatives without damaging vitality. *Colour was his guide.* Whether he was right or wrong, I do not give an opinion."

Seemingly red is the most difficult and elusive colouring to perpetuate. Frequently reds are produced from the mating of two self-coloured specimens, and will turn up occasionally, though in small numbers, in the litters where both sire and dam were blacks.

Since the first edition of this book was published, however, reds have become much more easily produced, thanks in a great measure to imported American and Canadian blood, and to-day it is more the exception than the rule to produce from two red parents colours other than those of the parents.

A well-known breeder, previously referred to in the chapter on strains, Mr. R. de C. Peele, once summarised his experiences in the attempt to produce reds. As the matter is one of general interest, I take the liberty of reproducing his remarks, as follows:—

"Referring to the colour question in Cockers, my experience with regard to reds is certainly peculiar. On three different occasions I have bred whole-coloured reds from the union of a blue roan and a black, and though I have on many occasions bred from these reds with blue roans, I have never bred a red, or heard of a red having been bred in this way. The colour seems to crop up when least expected in a very mysterious way, and to disappear again just as suddenly when you attempt to perpetuate it. How does the colour arise, and why are the dogs generally whole-reds and not red-roans?"

The following shows in tabulated form the result of the experiment alluded to by Mr. Peele, as given in *Our Dogs:*

Sire	Dam	Colour of Puppies
Rivington Bluecoat (blue roan) (Rio—Beauty III)	A.K.C. (Canadian-bred black) (Black Dufferin—Little Lady)	3 black, 1 red, and 1 red and white
George Bowdler (black) (Tim Obo—Batchcott Rose)	Braeside Betty (blue roan) (Welford Duke—Milstone Duchess)	4 reds
Braeside Bustle (blue roan) (Viceroy—Braeside Bizz)	Rouge Bowdler (whole red) (Rivington Bluecoat—A.K.C.)	2 black
Blue Peter (blue roan) Braeside Bustle—B. Betty)	Judy Bowdler (black and tan) (Braeside Bob—Phyllis Bowdler)	2 black and tan and 1 red

Tabulated details of more recent date give some very interesting data on the colour question.

Litter	Sire	Dam	Colour of Puppies
1st litter	Church Leigh Stormer (blue roan) Ch. Invader of Ware (blue roan) ex Church Leigh Bess (liver roan)	Blythe Snuff (liver) (Church Leigh Royalist (liver and white) ex Blythe Black Susan, black and of all black breeding)	2 blue roans 2 liver and white 2 solid blacks, 2 solid livers
2nd litter	Church Leigh Druid (black) (Dominorum Druid (blue roan) ex Belle of Sauls) (black)	Blythe Snuff (see above)	1 black 5 mis-marked blacks, 1 black and white
3rd litter	Dominorum D'Arcy (black) (by Corn Crake, black roan ex Dominorum Diana, black)	Blythe Snuff (see above)	3 blue roans, 1 black and white, 3 solid blacks
1st litter	Fulmer Bustle (blue roan) (Fairholme Rally, blue roan ex Fulmer Magpie, black and white)	Langmoor Vexation (blue) (Pinbrook Sandboy, red ex Langmoor Flora, liver roan)	2 blue roans
2nd litter	Ch. Invader of Ware (blue roan) (Drumraney Gunner, blue roan ex Drumraney Wonder, black roan)	L. Vexation	5 blue roans, 1 black and white, 1 lemon roan
3rd litter	Ch. Invader of Ware	L. Vexation	3 blue roans, 2 black and white, 2 lemon roans
4th litter	Ch. Invader of Ware	L. Vexation	4 blue roans, 1 black and white, 2 lemon roans
5th litter	Ch. Joyful Joe (blue roan) (Cobnar Critic, black roan ex Dore Moor Jennie, black roan)	L. Vexation	2 blue roans, 4 liver roans, 1 lemon roan
6th litter	Blaedown Bang (blue roan) (Ch. Invader of Ware, blue roan ex Bampton Nora, black and white)	L. Vexation	4 blue roans*

Litter	Sire	Dam	Colour of Puppies
1st litter	Boy of Fittleworth (blue roan) (Rosemount Spot, blue roan ex Rosemount Peggy black roan)	Falconer's Cowslip (black and white) (Ch. Invader of Ware, blue roan ex Ch. Exquisite of Ware, black, white, and tan)	4 black and white, 5 blue roans
2nd litter	Cobnar Critic (blue roan) (Southernwood Critic, blue roan ex Falconer's Spangle, blue roan)	Falconer's Cowslip	5 blue roan, 4 liver roan
3rd litter	Cobnar Critic	F. Cowslip	6 blue roan, 3 liver roan
4th litter	Freelance of Ware (blue roan) (Fairholme Rally, blue roan ex Country Girl, blue roan)	F. Cowslip	4 blue roan, 1 blue roan and tan, 2 black, white, and tan, 1 black and white, white, and tan, 1 liver roan and tan

*A bitch from this litter mated to Ch. Invader of Ware (blue roan) produced two lemon roans.

Tri-colours, a few years ago, were quite a craze, but do not appear to have survived the war period (when breeding was restricted) in great numbers. After all, this is not a matter for much regret, as so many of the specimens were lacking in richness of colouring. The blue roan and tan gave a somewhat foreign appearance to their possessors, but the liver roans and tans harmonised better, and several beautifully coloured specimens with these markings were produced. More black, white and tans are again in this year of grace cropping up and almost without exception show great quality.

ROWCLIFFE MIRACLE MAID
(U.S.A. Bred)

Lemon roans are now in considerable vogue, but with this colouring there is always a tendency to flesh-coloured noses and light eyes.

The texture of coat in both the tri-colours and lemon roans, curiously enough, generally appears to be of greater quality and better texture than any colour.

E. A. WILLING, *the first President of the new American English Cocker Spaniel Club*

Liver or red roans are becoming more popular, and a really good one of this colouring, with nose and eye in harmony, presents a very attractive appearance. It is to be noted, though, that the coats of liver or red roans require much more attention than blue roans when preparing for exhibition. Frequently, too, many of this colouring (liver or red) grow a soft lint coat.

The introduction of blacks is, in my opinion, highly desirable to maintain a common standard of type for the two groups. It should be remembered, however, that black is a primary colour and usually exerts a greater influence in the pigmentary process. For example, a black and blue roan when mated will generally result in " foul " marked blacks, which may be of little value for show purposes, though unsurpassed as breeding stock.

The type in reds is now almost on a par with the best of the other colours, and the greatest credit is due to the post-war breeders who have devoted their energies in this direction

146

with the most excellent results. The best reds, however, bred up to date have usually a cross of the best blood of other colours close up in their pedigrees, and the influence of imported American stock, as I said previously, has done much to establish the colour.

BROADCASTER OF WARE [*Hedges, Lytham*
(Imported, Canadian)

THE DESCRIPTIVE STANDARD OF THE COCKER SPANIEL

HEAD.—A nicely-developed square muzzle and jaw, with distinct stop. Skull and forehead should be well developed, with plenty of room for brain power, cleanly chiselled and not cheeky.

EYES.—Full, but not prominent, hazel or brown coloured, harmonising with colour or coat, with a general expression of intelligence and gentleness. decidedly wide-awake, bright, and merry.

EARS.—Lobular, set on low, leather fine and not extending beyond the nose, well clothed with long silky hair, which should be straight—no positive curls or ringlets.

NECK.—Long, strong and muscular, and neatly set on to fine sloping shoulders.

BODY (including Size and Symmetry).—Compact and firmly knit together, giving the impression of a concentration of power and untiring activity; the total weight should be about 25 lb. to 28 lb.

NOSE.—Sufficiently wide and well-developed to ensure the exquisite scenting power of this breed.

SHOULDERS AND CHEST.—The former sloping and fine, chest deep and well developed, but not too wide and round to interfere with the free action of the forelegs.

Photo]   CHAMPION MIDRIFF MIRACLE MAN   [*Tauskey*
(Black and White, American Bred)

BACK AND LOIN.—Short in back. Immensely strong and compact in proportion to the size and weight of the dog; slightly drooping towards the tail.

HIND QUARTERS.—Wide, well rounded, and very muscular.

STERN.—That most characteristic of blue blood in all the Spaniel family may, in the lighter and more active Cocker, although set low down, be allowed a slighter higher carriage than in the other breeds, but never cocked up over, but rather in a line with the back, although the lower the carriage and action the better, and when at work its action should be incessant in this, the brightest and merriest of the whole Spaniel family. Not docked too short.

FEET AND LEGS.—The legs must be well boned, feathered and straight, for the tremendous exertions expected from this grand little sporting dog, and should be sufficiently short for concentrated power, but not too short as to interfere with its full activity. Feet firm, round, and cat-like, not too large or spreading or loose jointed.

CHAMPION GOLFHILL ECLIPSE (Black)

COAT.—Flat and silky in texture, never wiry nor wavy, with sufficient feather; but not too profuse, and never curly.

COLOUR.—Various; in self colours a white shirt frill is most undesirable; white feet should not be allowed in any specimen of self-colour.

GENERAL APPEARANCE.—That of an active, merry sporting dog. The Cocker Spaniel does not follow on the lines of the larger Field Spaniel, either in lengthiness, lowness, or otherwise, but is shorter in back, and rather higher on the legs.

SCALE OF POINTS FOR JUDGING COCKER SPANIELS

Positive Points.

Head and Jaws	10
Eyes	5
Ears	5
Neck	10
Body	20
Fore-legs	10
Hind-legs	10
Feet	10
Stern	10
Coat and Feather	10
Total Positive Points ...	100

Negative Points.

Light Eyes	10
Light Nose	15
Hair Curled on Ears (very undesirable)	15
Coat (curly, woolly, or wiry)	20
Carriage of Stern	20
Top Knot	20
Total Negative Points ...	100

THE ENGLISH COCKER IN AMERICA

The Cocker was founded in America almost entirely on exports from Mr. J. J. Farrow's " Obo " Kennel, Obos such as Lily, Tim, Frank, and Betty all contributing largely to the building up of the breed, and were at a little later date materially assisted by the importation into America of Mr. J. M. Porter's coloured dog, Braeside Bob. In those days Cockers were long and low in type, weighed around 20 lbs., and measured 10 to 12 inches at shoulder.

The American breeder has to a great extent stuck rigidly to a small dog, the standard for many years being fixed at 25 lbs., a yoke that the English Cocker breeder broke away from nearly half a century ago, and the abandonment of this inflexible rule saw the rapid improvement here in the Cocker as a working dog.

Many Cockers leaving this country for America during the last twenty years have been exhibited there, but owing to the great gulf that divided them, particularly in size, received little recognition in the show ring.

A year or two ago several sporting owners got together with the result that, thanks to their efforts to obtain recognition for the English type, the American Kennel Club now cater for them, the Gilbertian position having arisen that two separate classifications are arranged, the one designated as "American type Cockers," the other "English Cockers"; it is considered the thin end of the wedge, and it is sincerely hoped by American enthusiasts that the A.K.C. will go further and make a separate breed of the English Cocker. I believe there is a " feeling " that it would be wrong for the two to be inter-bred. The situation as it at present exists is ably summed up by an article which appeared in the Cocker Spaniel Club Year Book from the pen of Mr. Homer Hendricks, the Hon. Secretary of the English Cocker Spaniel Club of America.

" THE ENGLISH COCKER IN AMERICA

" 'English Cockers' have made remarkable progress in America as a result of the action which the American Kennel Club took in May, 1936, recognising them as a separate variety in the Cocker Spaniel breed. Prior to that time it was well nigh foolish to exhibit an English Cocker at any of the recognised shows, for the competition was in the same class as the American-type Cockers, and as all were judged according to the American-type standard, the judges almost invariably put the English Cockers 'down' and the American Cockers 'up.'

" The new arrangement has, on the whole, proved not unsatisfactory. However, it is to be hoped that the American Kennel Club will eventually declare the English Cocker a separate breed as distinguished from a variety of the same breed as American-type Cockers.

" Following the action of the Kennel Club recognising the English Cocker, a sanctioned match for English Cockers exclusively was held, June 20th, 1936, on the farm of Mr. and Mrs. E. S. Willing, in Chester County, Pa., and this was also the occasion for the formal organisation of the English Cocker Spaniel Club of America. The Club has been active and it has enjoyed splendid growth. At the time this is written (August, 1938) it has sixty-seven members, and among them are some of the most prominent dog fanciers in America.

*　　*　　*　　*　　*　　*

" It is a pleasure to announce that during the year an American-bred English Cocker has attained his Championship. This honour has gone to Miss Doris Flagg's The Laird of Uxbridge (by Ch. Surmise of Ware—Ch. Miss Trilby of Ware).

" The judging of English Cockers in this country has been somewhat unsatisfactory, due to the scarcity of qualified judges who are familiar with the English type. In order to remedy this situation, the English Cocker Spaniel Club is encouraging its members to apply for licences to judge, and it is encouraging the larger shows to use judges which the Club approves.

" Our American-bred English Cockers, we regret to say, are not as good as the better dogs which are imported. But if you will continue to furnish us with good breeding stock (especially do we need good bitches), we venture to say that dogs of our breeding will be better and better in the course of time.

" In any event, the English Cocker can look forward to a great future in America. A larger, more active, and true sporting-type Cocker is needed here; the English Cocker meets those requirements, and with the sponsorship which it has in this country there can be no question that it will continue to make rapid progress.

HOMER HENDRICKS,

Secretary, English Cocker Spaniel
Club of America."

Canada has progressed faster than the U.S.A. and has already given separate status to the English Cocker, with the result that for " best in group " competition both the English and American type are represented.

There seems little doubt that the English type will make rapid strides in America, as his suitability by his slightly increased size to perform his legitimate work will prove a great factor in his favour.

152

CHAPTER V

How nicely you brought him, unruffled each feather,
Just as he lay on the bracken or heather;
He was rather a mouthful, but you don't care,
I believe you would struggle along with a hare.
                                        Brown.

THE COCKER SPANIEL AS A GUNDOG

EARLY TRAINING FOR SPORT
AND FIELD TRIALS

FIELD Trials for Spaniels—The Woodcock Spaniel—Improvement of Working Qualities—Championship Stake for Cockers—Game Finding—Retrieving—First Principles of Training—Selecting a Puppy for Training—Working to Signals—Ranging—Training with a "Dummy"—Working Up-wind—Hunting and Questing—Flushing the Game—"Foot" Scent and "Blood" Scent—Gun Shyness—Training on Live Rabbits—The Check Card—Dropping to Fur—Dropping to Shot—Don'ts for Trainers—List of Kennel Club Challenge Certificate Winners from 1910 to 1931 inclusive—List of Champion Cocker Spaniels (post-war period)—Field Trial Champion Cocker Spaniels.

FIELD trials for Spaniels have existed for nearly a quarter of a century, and of recent years Cockers have played a conspicuous part, having been the recipients of numerous awards in any variety competition. In an article written by Mr. C. A. Phillips for the 1923 Year Book of the Cocker Spaniel Club, a well-deserved tribute is paid to the breed, for Mr. Phillips traced the pedigrees of several winners of the English Springer variety, and in doing so proves that these had more than a passing relationship with the Cocker.

A reference to the history of the Cocker Spaniel (*vide* Chapter I) and to the older sporting works on the breed, will show it to be depicted as a Woodcock Spaniel, and used for flushing these elusive birds from their haunts, which the other members of the Spaniel family found too dense and difficult to penetrate. Since those days the Cocker has fallen into line with the Springer, inasmuch

View of Cocker Spaniel Club's Field Trials Held in Scotland

he is now called upon not only to flush his game, but to retrieve it to hand. The result is, with all things taken into consideration, the field work of the Cocker to-day compares most favourably with that of any other gundog; in fact, at recent trials in stakes confined to Cockers, the work was pronounced by experts to be more uniformly good than that witnessed in the events restricted to other breeds.

F.T. Ch. Elibank Attention
Winner of the first K.C. Cocker Field Trial Championship.

For his size, the Cocker has indubitably proved his capacity and courage for all work in the field that can possibly be asked of a Spaniel.

The improvement of working qualities in the breed since the war cannot fail to enhance the enthusiasm of his admirers. The field trial movement, too, has assumed considerable dimensions, for in the first post-war trials the stakes for Cockers attracted very little competition, but last season no fewer than twenty-three Cocker Spaniels competed in the Kennel Club Championship Stake, and it may be truly said all were very good gundogs. The movement is yet in its infancy, but Cocker Spaniel owners may rest assured that their breed is capable of not only maintaining the position it has already achieved, but will be surpassed by none in these competitive tests of skill in the field.

The fact that the Kennel Club have allotted a championship stake for Cocker Spaniels is testimony to the progress the breed has made, and will tend further to increase its popularity among field triallers and as a canine aid to the shooting man.

It should always be remembered that the primary duty of any Spaniel, irrespective of breed, is *game finding*, and that retrieving in comparison is of secondary importance. Without questing and hunting, combined with the courage to face punishing cover, little game would be found for the gun.

It is urged against the Cocker that he is incapable of retrieving a weighty hare, but his traducers forget how very infrequently, when following his legitimate vocation, the Cocker or any other breed is called upon to accomplish this task. Many Cockers can and will do it readily and in good style; others, again, find the weighty burden too much for them, yet any well-trained Cocker will take the line of a hare, find the game and drag it from thick cover, reeds, or bramble. This performance should surely suffice for the needs of the ordinary shooting man, as few hares are shot that could not be picked up by hand.

SOME FIRST PRINCIPLES IN TRAINING

Undoubtedly the early lessons in training are by far the most important, and a puppy can be easily marred by wrong treatment at the very outset. *Patience, patience, and patience,* combined with an equable temperament, are essential qualities in the successful trainer. Without patience, which is sure to be tried to its utmost by almost every dog passing through his hands, success can never be attained. Hand breaking, as it is termed, can be carried on indoors, and in this case it is necessary—as it is throughout the training—the pupil should be given the undivided attention of the trainer, with all counter-attractions removed from the spot. One of the most successful trainers of modern times, an amateur unrivalled in this sphere of work, states that, in his opinion, his successes are due to the constant association with his pupil and that all the elementary lessons are given indoors or in a garden.

FIELD TRIAL CH. SIMON OF CORRAN
(Orange and White)
Owned by the late Hon. R. W. Bingham (The late American Ambassador)

In selecting a puppy for training for field work, every opportunity should be taken of observing if the prospective performer is bold or shy, whether he is capable of thinking for himself and possesses initiative and the questing or hunting instinct. When observing a litter of puppies it can be quickly ascertained which one shows the greatest boldness, activity, and initiative.

When you have made your selection do not make the mistake of starting the puppy's training at too early an age. I hold to the opinion that every puppy requires " a

157

playtime " in the same way as a child, and that to start his education before his mental and physical powers are developed sufficiently to cope with the lessons only leads to weariness and ultimate disgust at being called upon to perform tasks which a few months later he will do readily. Experience has shown that to first try the pupils out on ground where rabbits are certain to be found lying out, and when disturbed make for heavy cover such as blackthorn, briars, etc., is the best method to encourage courageous hunting in cover. The puppy should be indulged in his hunting for several days; restraint can come afterwards when once his handler feels convinced that he has the requisite courage and " drive " so essential in a genuine gundog. Nevertheless, at from six to seven months the pupil may be encouraged to use his nose by trailing toothsome morsels dragged over the ground with a string or cord; even so, the lessons must be discontinued when the puppy displays the first sign of weariness or lack of attention. The early education should consist of teaching the pupil to know his name and answer to it unhesitatingly. To do this his confidence must be gained, for without the existence of confidence in his tutor, results will be negligible. Chastisement, rather than tending to mitigate a fault for which he was castigated, intensifies it, especially in the case of a more than ordinary sensitive individual. Usually the fault, instead of lying with the dog, is with the owner, who is incapable of inculcating and imparting the lessons. Teach the pupil to sit down or drop, to come to heel, and when galloping around on his own to immediately respond when whistled or called by name. To impart the " drop," the trainer should stand over the puppy and gently press it to the ground, saying kindly but firmly at the same time, " Drop " or " Hup." Most likely the pupil will roll on its back and raise all four legs in the air in a most beseeching manner. Patience must be brought into play, and when the puppy is again on its legs repeat the process until he realises what is required. When this is achieved and the youngster will readily drop at command, move away for a few paces and again give the order. The pupil will most likely endeavour to follow with the thought that he must " drop " near to, or at the handler's feet. This must be corrected, and he should be taken back to the original spot and the command repeated, all attempts to move being checked. It is a good plan to raise the right arm with the palm of the hand towards the pupil, fingers extended, when giving the command. The distance may then be gradually increased, as likewise the duration period the pupil is kept in the " dropped " position, until he will remain steadily in that posture in the far corner of the garden or field, or check his headlong return by " dropping " on perceiving the raised hand. Care must be taken not to tire or surfeit him. A few minutes daily

F.T. Ch. Auchencairn Jasper

will suffice at first, and each satisfactory performance should be rewarded by the gift of a tit-bit or dainty morsel. Should his attention be distracted or his interest wane, then leave off the lesson, return him to the kennel, and re-start when the counter-attraction has been removed or his interest in the game returns. Try to interest him in the same way you would a child, remembering that the analogy may be carried further and that, childlike, he soon tires. Therefore, make the lessons short, yet frequent.

The training process will be considerably facilitated if the trainer makes it a point to look after his charge himself, exercising it, feeding, bedding down, and in every way associating with it all the time possible. It is by this constant association that the dog in time recognises that certain words mean certain requirements, and comes to know the tones of the voice. It is by these tones he chiefly interprets his trainer's wishes. An encouraging inflection when approval is merited, and a vibrant, sharply-spoken word for correction, will be readily discriminated and meet with instant response. Above all, never shout at, or unduly raise the voice during the lessons; the quieter the commands are given, the better and more promptly will desired results be achieved. Always use the same word—a short, simple one is best— when giving the order; never vary this, and as the education progresses the spoken word may be accompanied by a definite signal of the arm or hand, differently made for each requirement, until the pupil will work almost entirely to signals without the need for the trainer to use his voice. This silent or semi-silent system of handling working dogs has everything in its favour. How frequently during the past few years have we seen the chances of a really good dog of winning a field trial completely marred by an otherwise competent trainer shouting command after command at his charge until the bewildered animal, not knowing what is expected of him, has finally given in and done nothing. Happily, the ways of the old school of " breakers " have been replaced by more intelligent methods, and though occasionally at trials one or two handlers—and professionals at that—display an incapacity to control their charges through lack of self-control themselves, there is considerably less of that excitable shouting at and running around after their dogs than was formerly the case.

RANGING AND RETRIEVING

These two traits are almost instinctively possessed by all Cocker Spaniels whose forebears were derived from a bold strain. Occasionally they will be found lacking, and in other cases, if not apparent, may be readily instilled and developed. If the pupil is backward, the example of a trained and older dog may produce the desired result. First of all, try the pupil with a " dummy ' thrown a few yards. " Drop " him first, and after the lapse of a few moments send him for it. If he goes after it and brings it back to hand, well and good. Should he ignore the command and make no attempt to retrieve, then " drop " him, or, better still, confine him to a run whence he can, in plain view, witness the finished performance of the older dog. When he has become interested and is jealously desirous of exhibiting his own prowess in this new game, release him from the run and continue with the lessons, the distance the " dummy " is thrown

FIELD TRIAL MEETING, SEPTEMBER 1938

being increased as the drill progresses. When he has picked up the " dummy," encourage him to return with it quickly. If you turn your back on him and walk away, he will hurry through fear of your leaving him. If you stand still facing him, and addressing to him such remarks as " Good dog," " Bring it," etc., he will probably think you are encouraging him to play with the " dummy " or that he is being lauded for carrying it about.

Always remember to " drop " the pupil and keep him in that position for some moments ere sending him to retrieve, otherwise you may implant the seeds of what is a serious defect in any dog used as an aid to the gun, viz., "running in."

Having returned with the "dummy," never snatch it from his mouth; allow him to proudly retain it for a moment or so while you show your approval by a caress, then encourage him to gently surrender it to your hand.

During these early stages live birds or rabbits should not be used, only the "dummy," which may be made

FIELD TRIAL FOLLOWERS AND COMPETITORS

from an old glove or a rabbit skin, stuffed with hay or wool. The "dummy" should be removed when the lesson is over, and never left lying around within access of the pupil, otherwise he may, puppy-like, run off with it and proceed to tear it to pieces, a circumstance, which, if not checked—and here, as in other cases, prevention is better than cure—may lead to disastrous consequences when in course of time our promising candidate for field trial honours is introduced to "game," either fur or feather

For this reason any tendency to worry or " mouth " the " dummy," when sent to retrieve it, should be immediately checked.

Concentration by both the trainer and his charge on the work in hand is indispensable. Any slackening on the part of either should be the signal for the lesson to be adjourned. We know, comparatively speaking, very little about the psychology of the canine, but we do know that certain persons are the happy possessors of gifts—call it personality, magnetism, or what you will—that enable them to obtain implicit and instant obedience from members of the canine race. Some possess this in higher degree than others, while in many it is either totally absent or if inherent has become atrophied through want of use. Much

F.T. CH. TORNADO OF WARE
Winner of the Field Trial Championship

can be done towards acquiring or increasing this power, and the trainer who concentrates his whole mind on the object to be achieved, mentally saying to himself: " I will you to do this," " or that," at the same time summoning the reserve of power within him and sending it out direct to his charge accompanied by the command, will find the latter surprisingly receptive and amenable to this influence. Success will not come all at once, but the practice is more than worth while.

When the pupil is proficient in retrieving the thrown " dummy," he may next be tried in finding that article when hidden in long grass or bushes. For this lesson he may be taken into a field, or open space, or common, and should, at first, always be worked *up-wind.* He should never be allowed to observe the process of hiding the article, and it is preferable that this should be done by an assistant, entering the field from the far side to prevent the puppy from foot-scenting his trainer's trail to the hidden article. The reason the puppy should not see the article hidden is, that otherwise he would " hunt by eye " and make straight for the spot, without calling upon his olfactory organs to assist him in the search. One cannot make a dog use his nose, but only encourage him to use it.

F.T. Ch. Pat of Chrishall
One of the greatest Field Trial Sires of all times,
photographed in his old age

It is to be remembered that a Spaniel when he has located the game, be it a rabbit or pheasant, is required to flush or dislodge it and to remain steady (i.e., not to chase) to its going away. This is a test of steadiness and a temptation almost as great as any that could be given to any animal. When shot at and possibly wounded the game may run, so that in order to become a finished worker the Spaniel must early learn to differentiate between " live foot " scent and " blood " scent. He is expected to push a rabbit from its seat, to remain steady,

164

evincing no inclination to chase or pursue it, and, if the fur is missed by the gun, escaping unscathed, the Spaniel must continue questing for other game as if the first temptation had never presented itself. On the other hand, if the rabbit is killed, or crawls away wounded, the dog must comprehend from the command given him that he is to either follow the line of the wounded or dead game and retrieve it to hand, or remain steady while the game, if within easy distance of the gun, may be picked up by the later or his loader. It will be thus seen that throughout his working life implicit and instant obedience must be rendered to the words of command taught to and comprehended by the Spaniel during his early training. It is a fatal mistake on the part of a trainer—or by anyone who has to do with the animals—to look upon and consider their working field dogs as merely game-finding and retrieving machines. Every canine has an individuality of its own—little traits, habits and idiosyncrasies—and it is only by a careful study of these that he can be prevailed upon to give of his best; in other words, the control of the dog's bodily actions and movements can only be effected through the medium of and impressions conveyed to his mind.

If an enclosed rabbit warren or pen is available the puppy may now be introduced to live game and allowed to push out rabbits from their seats. It is assumed that the handler has already equipped himself with a firearm and some blank cartridges and that the pupil has become indifferent to the actual report of the gun. This may be accomplished by accustoming the puppy to the noise by discharging the weapon, first at some distance, which should be gradually decreased, until he will stand unmoved at the heels of the shooter. Should he display any nervousness at the unusual report, a good plan is to get an assistant to discharge the weapon at a distance, the trainer meanwhile encouraging the puppy and distracting its attention by making much of it. The discharge of the gun or a similar loud report may be given as a signal for meal times until all traces of nervousness are dispelled and the puppy comes to look upon the bang with eager antici- pation as a gratifying summons to dinner. Gun-shyness, once acquired, is difficult to eradicate, and as a gun-shy dog is worse than useless for the shooting man, every care must be taken when imparting this all-important lesson. A cure suggested for gun-shy or nervous dogs is to allow them to chase a rabbit a time or two and to shoot over them at the instant that their minds are diverted. The companionship of a trained dog during this part of the puppy's education will inspire confidence in the youngster and greatly expedite the desired result.

Having introduced the pupil to the pen of live rabbits, the attractions of their scent will soon become manifest in the demeanour of the youngster, the hunting instinct

F. T. Ch. Banchory Rachael
Winner of the K.C. Field Trial Championship

will assert itself and he will soon be merrily engaged in puzzling out or following the line or trail of the game. When he comes up to and dislodges his quarry, the pupil should be " dropped." Should he ignore the command and display a tendency to chase the running rabbit, the check-cord must be utilised. This is a length of stout cord —window cord will do—about 20 yards in length, one end of which is fastened to the pupil's collar and the other allowed to trail loosely over the ground. All attempts by the puppy to chase his game can be checked by the trainer placing his foot on the loose end of the cord, thus bringing the pupil to an abrupt halt. He will soon realise from the discomfort inflicted by the jerk of the cord what is required. Let him remain in the dropped position for a couple of minutes, then give the order " gone away " and start him hunting in another direction. When he is proficient in dropping to fur, lessons in dropping to shot may be given. Here, again, the check cord will probably be required, for it is quite a different

INT. CH. BARNEY OF WARE [*Fall*
(Field Trials)
Winner of the Championship Field Trial Stakes—England and India

matter for the pup'l to see a rabbit going away untouched and for him to stand steady and unmoved when the tempting quarry is bowled over and lies spasmodically kicking within a few yards of his nose. Leave the dog at the " drop," checking any inclination to move by the raised arm signal coupled with the usual word of command, or by stepping on the check cord. When he is quite steadied, go and pick up the rabbit yourself. Repeat this lesson two or three times. The reason for picking up the rabbit by hand is that the pupil must be brought to clearly understand that he is *not to retrieve every " kill,"* but only when ordered to do so. Many beginners make the mistake of sending the dog to retrieve each and every object killed or thought to have been killed, with the result that the pupil soon associates the discharge of the weapon with the act of retrieving, and " runs in " to the shot without waiting for the order to retrieve. Encourage the puppy to " stand " to his rabbits, and when

Photo]   Champion Sand Spring Surmise   [Tauskey
(Dark Red, American Bred)

he is drawing near to them be sure that the loose end of the check-cord is within reach, so that when the rabbit bolts and the puppy is disposed to follow, you can immediately check the attempt. If the quarry refuses to be dislodged—frequently they will not move until the dog is less than a foot distant—go up yourself, " drop " the dog, and pick up the rabbit. Keep the pupil in the dropped position for a few minutes, for it is by such lessons steadiness is inculcated.

The pupil may behave perfectly when inside the pen or enclosure, but outside, with the greater range and freedom, will probably take liberties. If so, the use of the check-cord must be again requisitioned. For the puppy's first retrieve a half-grown rabbit should be selected and the pupil should be given his task while the rabbit is yet warm. For his first retrieve the rabbit should have been cleanly killed, as a " squealer " or " legged " one may induce the puppy in the excitement of capture to " nip " or bite the game.

Exactly the same principles are applicable to the finding and retrieving of feather game, and if the rudiments here laid down are adopted, the beginner should have no

Photo]   CHAMPION SAND SPRING STORM CLOUD   [*Tauskey*
(American Bred)

difficulty in bringing his puppy's education to a successful conclusion. It is manifest that in a monograph of this nature, treating of different aspects of the popular Cocker Spaniel, it is impossible to devote more than a small space to the subject—one with which a volume could be filled—given at the head of this chapter.

To those, therefore, who would pursue the subject further with a view to their dogs competing in first-class company at the principal field trial meetings, I have no hesitation in strongly recommending that valuable work, *Spaniels: Their Breaking for Sport and Field Trials*, by the late H. W. Carlton. It is a book that amateur and professional trainer alike will find of absorbing interest, and to be of great value and profit to all concerned in the working abilities and qualities of the Spaniel family.

Finally, I would again emphasise that the trainer must possess a level, equable temperament, combined with the patience of Job; that no lesson should be persevered with when it becomes apparent that either tutor or pupil are out of harmony with each other; and that concentration by both of them on the work in hand is the first and primary essential towards success.

In respect of his working abilities, your dog is what you have made him, neither more nor less.

Never punish your dog unless he clearly understands why. If there is any doubt in the matter, give him the benefit of it. The late Mr. Wm. Arkwright wrote: " To a Spaniel's character incessant thrashings are fatal, as under such treatment he becomes either cowed or case-hardened, according to his individual temperament, but never broken."

Gain your dog's confidence, associate with him all you can. You will never make a willing servant of a dog which is suspicious of you.

Constant observation of his individual traits and peculiarities will well repay.

Insist upon obedience; never give an order without seeing that it is obeyed.

Never continue with a lesson when the pupil has lost interest.

Never lose your temper with a puppy, or any dog, for that matter.

Avoid shouting at your dog. It is rarely necessary and never at a well-trained one.

Do *not* send him to retrieve everything you kill.

Do *not* shoot at game your dog has found unless he " drops."

Do *not* shoot near to your dog when he is hunting or retrieving—a chance pellet or ricochet may undo all your work.

CHALLENGE CERTIFICATE WINNERS, 1910-1939

The following is a complete list of Challenge Certificate winners for the years 1910 to 1939 (inclusive), as recorded in the K.C.S.B. It will be observed that during this period of the total number of dogs recorded in this list 82 were blacks and 129 of a colouring other than black.

CHAMPION WILFUL WARRIOR (French Bred)

BEAU BOWDLER (809P), sire Ch. Bob Bowdler—Ch. Shepperton Bluebell, born Sept. 25th, 1908; black and white.
CH. BELWELL SURPRISE (812P), Arabian Sam—Arab Phloss, born Sept. 12th, 1908; black and white.
BRUTON TED (817P), Brunswick Ladas—Bruton Princess, born April 25th, 1907; black.
CH. DOONY BLACKIE (1083L), Heir Apparent—Doony Pride, born June 8th, 1905; black.

171

CH. DOONY DUSK (821P), Heir Apparent, Doony Pride, born Jan. 18th, 1909; black.

NOLL OF HARTING (820P), Ch. Dixon Bowdler—Crackle Bowdler, born Aug. 4th, 1908; blue roan.

CH. RIVINGTON ROGUE (1007N), Hampton Guard—Rivington Arrow, July 13th, 1907; black.

CIPPENHAM GLITTER (988N), Heir Apparent—Gipsy of Ware, Dec. 7th, 1908; black.

CH. DOONY BETTY (990N), Trafalgar Ben—Judith of Greeta, July 30th, 1908; blue roan.

CH. EVELYN BOWDLER (802Q), Ch. Dixon Bowdler—Amie of Ware, Aug. 29th, 1907; blue roan.

CH. JETSAM BOWDLER (1243J), Pax—Bess, May, 1903; black.

CH. RIVINGTON PRIDE (830P), Rivington Boy—Rivington Peggie, July 20th, 1908; liver roan.

CH. ROCKLYN BETTY (810Q), Joe of Bobeva—Knocka Bluebell, Dec. 4th, 1908; blue roan.

BETHAM BEN (243Q), Ch. Doony Swell—Warburton Ladybird, Sept. 9th, 1909; black and white.

COURTFIELD JOHN (846R), Ch. Doony Swell—Ch. Truth, Aug. 3rd, 1909; blue roan.

GRINDON GERALD (178R), Ch. Braeside Rival—Grindon Mary, July 27th, 1910; blue roan.

CH. RIVINGTON GUNNER (481M), Ch. Doony Swell—Ch. Rivington Ruth, June 22nd, 1906; blue roan.

BEVEL BOWDLER (839R), Beau Bowdler—Ch. Evelyn Bowdler, Oct. 10th, 1910; blue roan.

BRIGHT WITCH (814P), Wilton Lad—Arabian Doris, July 27th, 1907; black and tan.

GALTREES MAY (853R), Rivington Regent—Galtrees Nell, June 26th, 1910; black.

RIVINGTON HELEN (858R), Fielding Blueboy—Rivington Rose, July 31st, 1910; lemon, white, and roan.

TRUMPINGTON LADY (814Q), Ch. Rivington Rogue—Trumpington Lass, June 6th, 1909; black.

YSTWYTH SIREN (863R), Mike of St. Foy—Ch. Evelyn Bowdler, June 29th, 1909; blue roan.

DARGLE PINTO (847R), Monarch of Ware—Headfort Meg, Aug. 29th, 1910; black and white.

CH. HAMPTON MARQUIS (918S), Arlington Marquis—Doony Dora, Nov. 20th, 1910; black.

MASTER PERCY (1703L), Ch. Master Reuben—Mistress
Prue, April 19th, 1905; black.
ROCKLYN ARAB (340R), Arlington Marquis—Doony Dora,
Nov. 20th, 1910; black.
FAIRHOLME KATHLEEN (850R), Rivington Regent—
Galtrees Nell, June 8th, 1909; red.

CH. WILFUL WORSHIPPER
French Bred (Black)

FULMER MAGPIE (914S), Keynstone Pride—Floss, June
21st, 1910; black and white.
GALTREES FLORA (915S), Rivington Regent—Galtrees
Nell, June 26th, 1910; liver.

173

MINEMA (184s), Vivany Rupert—Clarencilla, June 2nd, 1910; black.

CH. RIVINGTON ROBENA (925s), Betham Ben—Rivington Rose, April 28th, 1911; black and white.

DOONY BLUE BOY (1086T), Ch. Doony Swell—Doony Bizz, May 9th, 1912; blue roan.

CH. DOONY BLUEBELL (1085T), Belwell Swell—Carrybridge Reminder, July 9th, 1911; blue roan.

DYRON'S SWELL (1378s), Belwell Swell—Dyron's Beauty, April 3rd, 1912; black and white.

RICKFORD ROOSEVELDT (1106T), Rickford Reuben—Rickford Rosalind, Aug. 26th, 1912; black.

RIVINGTON RAP (724R), Fielding Blueboy—Rivington Rose, July 31st, 1910; lemon and white.

STOUR SUCCESS (835P), Ch. Coony Blackie—Peggy's Pride, July 1st, 1908; black.

GAY BOWDLER (816s), Galtrees Raven—Blithe Bowdler, March 7th, 1912; black.

RADIUM OF WARE (1104T), Galtrees Raven—Blithe Bowdler, March 7th, 1912; black.

DURBAN GUNNER (1087T), Ch. Rivington Gunner—Durban Dinah, April 27th, 1912; black and white.

FULMER MAXIM (554v), Ch. Rivington Gunner—Fulmer Why, July 2nd, 1914; blue roan.

FULMER PEAT (838v), Ch. Hampton Marquis—Fulmer Jet, May 10th, 1913; black.

ROCKLYN MAGIC (168v), Rocklyn Rajah—Dunkeld Comet, July 14th, 1913; black.

FULMER JOANNA (835U), Ch. Dixon Bowdler—Fulmer June, April 27th, 1913; blue roan.

JOY BOWDLER (1096T), Ch. Doony Dusk—Ch. Jetsum Bowdler, June 11th, 1912; black.

CHELMSFORD CAUTION (262w), Rocklyn Magic—Dolly, Feb. 11th, 1915; black.

COLOUR CHARM (627w), Dyron's Bluecoat—Rocklyn Betsy, Oct. 25th, 1915; blue roan.

DOONY RIVAL (630w), Doony Major—Ch. Doony Bluebell, Aug. 1st, 1915; blue roan.

FULMER OVER (837U), Beau Bowdler—Fulmer Guess, June 15th, 1913; black and white.

FULMER ZULU (637w), Ch. Hampton Marquis—Sherington Fashion, Sept. 24th, 1915; black.

MONKERTON CHARLIE (11032), Galtrees Raven—Brookfield Gipsy, Jan. 8th, 1912; black and tan.

FAIRHOLME TYPE (530U), Belwell Swell—Carrybridge Reminder, Nov. 23rd, 1913; blue roan.

FAIRHOLME TYPIST (93V), Belwell Swell—Carrybridge Reminder, May 26th, 1915; blue roan.

FULMER MERRY (635W), Rocklyn Darkie—Rivington Runette, Aug. 9th, 1914; black.

TRUMPINGTON DAISY (854U), Adonis of Ware—Trumpington Pattie, Sept. 30th, 1912; black.

FULMER COUNTESS (225X), Fairholme Rally—Fulmer Duchess, June 29th, 1915; blue roan.

CHAMPION GOLDSTREAM GUARD OF CORDOVA
American Bred

COUSIN CONNIE (693AA), Corn Crake—Chiff Chaff, June 11th, 1919; liver roan.

FULMER BEN (700AA), Fairholme Rally—Fulmer Magpie, April 19th, 1916; blue roan.

FULMER KAFIR (240X), Ch. Hampton Marquis—Sherington Fashion, Sept. 24th, 1915; black.

CH. PINBROOK SCAMP (714AA), Dyron's Sambo—Brookfield Gipsy, July 19th, 1917; black.

FULMER BETTY (165Z), Fairholme Rally—Fulmer Magpie, March 13th, 1915; blue roan.

PEACEMAKER CF WARE (713AA), Hooe Gerald—Brad'ood Judy, April 16th, 1915; blue roan.

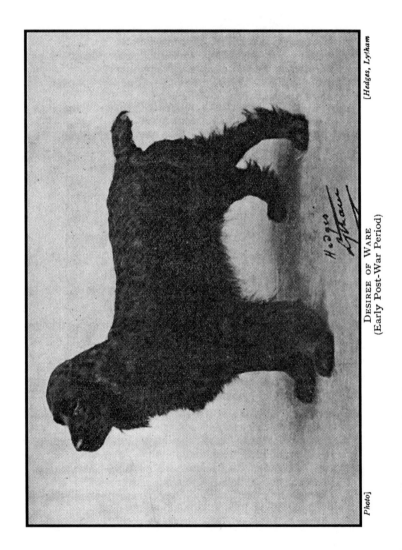

DESIREE OF WARE
(Early Post-War Period)

DESIREE OF WARE (695AA), Rocklyn Magic—Nettlecombe Bunty, May 4th, 1919; black.

REWARD OF THE GLORY (719AA), Rocklyn Blue Bottle—Fairholm Type, Aug. 14th, 1915; blue roan.

FLAWLESS OF WARE (699A), Stour Success—Devonshire Estelle, July 23rd, 1912; black.

STANDBURN LADY (723AA), Dunkeld Jock—Nell, Sept. 2nd, 1916; black.

FULMER BUSTLE (701AA), Fairholme Rally—Fulmer Magpie, April 19th, 1916; blue roan.

CH. REPTON ROSEMARY
(Australian Champion, Black and White)

FULMER GLEAM (702AA), Ch. Fulmer Peat—Sherington Fashion, Nov. 1st, 1919; black.

DYRON'S DANDY (241W), Ch. Doony Swell—Durban Dinah, March 31st, 1914; blue roan.

CH. IRRESISTIBLE OF WARE (458BB), Rocklyn Magic—Flawless of Ware; black.

ADMIRAL OF THE GLORY (805BB), Recorder of Ware—Nita of the Glory, Feb. 16th, 1920; black.

Captain Flint (51bb), Rocklyn Magic—Lady Betsy, Feb. 4th, 1920; black.

Helen's Glory (120x), Fulmer Peat—Helen of Ware, Aug. 15th, 1915; black.

Cashier of Ware (807bb), Recorder of Ware—Valerie, March 28th, 1920; black.

Durban Lady Nellie (696aa), Doony Major—Lassie McCaura, June 20th, 1919; blue roan.

Tantivy of Ware (1083cc), Falconer's Chittabob—Harriet of Ware, May 3rd, 1921; black.

Falconer's Spangle

Talent of Ware (1082cc), Rocklyn Magic—Newdigate Daisy, July 14th, 1921; black.

Langmoor Flora (1064cc), Fairholme Rally—Falconer's Cinders, April 26th, 1922; liver roan.

Foxham Madge (1049cc), Foxham Rally—Foxham Magpie, Aug. 25th, 1921; blue roan.

Timothy (1084cc), Fulmer Kafir—Wendy, June 13th, 1919; black.

Dominorum Dacia (1041cc), Rocklyn Magic—Hoyland Nell, Feb. 10th, 1920; black.

178

FALCONER'S SPANGLE (615cc), Fairholme Rally—Falconer's Tidy, Sept. 3rd, 1921; blue roan.

CORN COB (811B), Corn Crake—Rosemount Nellie, Sept. 19th, 1919; blue roan.

CORN CRAKE (692AA), Dyron's Bluecoat—Rocklyn Betsy, May 2nd, 1916; blue roan.

FULMER CHLOE (1051cc), Dandy—Dinah, June 28th, 1921; black.

DAPHNE OF DUNKERY (812BB), Fairholme Rally—Glamour of Ware, May 5th, 1920; liver roan.

FULMER BIDDY (820BB), Rickford Remus—Rickford Rosary, July 24th, 1917; black.

DUSK OF DUNKERY (1043cc), Lawyett—Craignethan, Blackie, June 1st, 1921; black.

FULMER DARKIE (416cc), Fulmer Zulu—Ashby Judy, March 8th, 1921; black.

MAVOURNEEN OF WARE (1068cc), Ottershaw Magic—Ottershaw Charmer, Feb. 3rd, 1919; black.

L'ILE BEAU BRUMMEL (254DD), Fulmer Ben—Silverwing of Felbrigg, Sept. 16th, 1921; black and white.

CHURCH LEIGH BESS (46DD), Corn Crake—Fairholme Ringlet, March 30th, 1921; liver roan.

EVERMERRY OF WARE (450DD), Fanfare of Ware—Rosebush, Oct. 13th, 1921; black.

SOUTHERNWOOD CRITIC (764DD), Corn Crake—Southernwood Peggy, May 27th, 1922; blue roan.

CH. TRUCE IN OFFALY (765DD), Rosemount Spot—Rosemount Beauty, May 13th, 1921; blue roan.

CH. INVADER OF WARE (1068DD), Drumreany Gunner—Drumreany Wonder, Sept. 6th, 1922; blue roan.

CARSPHAIRN DINAH (1166DD), Dunlop Darkie—Carsphairn Lena, April 18th, 1922; black.

ILLUMINATOR OF WARE (1257DD), Drumreany Gunner—Drumreany Wonder, Sept. 6th, 1922; blue roan.

HELEN'S BEAUTY (307BB), Adonis of Ware—Helen's Heiress, May 23rd, 1917; black.

FULMER ECLIPSE (777DD), Fulmer Darkie—Fulmer Gleam, Aug. 21st, 1922; black.

FOXHAM MAYPOLE (135EE), Foxham Top Hole—Foxham Magpie, Sept. 6th, 1922; liver roan.

THE KNUT (309EE), Ballywater Nigger—Nan, Feb. 15th, 1920; black.

GLORIA OF SAUL'S (1309DD), Footprint of Ware—Beauty's Girl, May 17th, 1922; black.

RIVINGTON RANTER (375EE), Rivington Saddle—Church Leigh Bess, June 11th, 1922; liver roan.

DOMINORUM DIANA (290EE), Driver of Ware—Dominorum DACIA, July 7th, 1922; black.

CH. EXQUISITE OF WARE (460EE), Freelance of Ware— Trix of Ogmore, June 27th, 1923; black, white, and tan.

Photo]   [*Hedges* Lytham
CH. IRREPRESSIBLE OF WARE
(Black)

WOLVERSHILL DUSK (501EE), Pinedale Perfection— Ivelton Dally, April 21st, 1923; black.

STORMCLOUD OF WARE (653EE), Ch. Pinbrook Scamp— Memoir of Ware, Jan. 1st, 1923; black.

FULMER REBECCA (1137EE), Fulmer Rob—Forbury Brenda, Aug. 25th, 1923; blue roan.

QUEENIE OF SAUL'S (594EE), Footprint of Ware—Beauty's Girl, May 17th, 1922; black.

FULMER DEFENDER (134EE), Cottesmore Rally—Fulmer Jessica, March 16th, 1923; blue roan.

DAZZLE OF DUNKERY (1778DD), Fairholme Rally—
Country Girl, Sept. 26th, 1922; blue roan.
CHURCH LEIGH RUBY (842EE), Corn Crake—Church Leigh
Velvet, May 13th, 1923; liver roan.
FOXHAM MINX (900EE), Corn Crake—Foxham Magpie,
April 3rd, 1923; black and white.
BLAEDOWN BUNTY, CH. (502EE), Ottershaw Clement—
Blaedown Lassie, June 3rd, 1923; black.
MANNEQUIN OF WARE (902EE), Ch. Pinbrook Scamp—
Memoir of Ware, Sept. 19th, 1923; black.
SLOGAN OF WARE (693EE), Indispensable of Ware—
Medallist of Ware, Sept. 30th, 1922; black.

Photo]   VIVARY CRUSADER   [*Fall*

DOMINORUM MICHAEL (654EE), Corn Crake—Miss Nibbs,
April 30th, 1923; blue roan.
BLUE BARBARA (747EE), Lawbro' Barbarian—Jan of
Sebright, May 7th, 1923; blue roan.
EMSLEA CORNFLOWER (74FF), Corn Crake (692AA)—
Foxham Magpie (819BB); blue roan.
IVER DANCER (150FF), Merry Buchanan (1109EE)—Azure
of Ware; black roan.
VIVARY CRUSADER (409FF), Invader of Ware, Ch. (1068DD)
—Merrivale Pawn; blue roan.

181

LANGMOOR VEXATION (531BB), Pinbrook Sandboy—Langmoor Flora; blue roan.

CHARLSTON AMBITION (573FF), Woodcut of Ware, Buzz Buzz; black.

FALCONER'S COWSLIP (801FF), Invader of Ware, Ch. (1068DD)—Exquisite of Ware, Ch. (460EE); black, white, and tan.

DASH O'MATHERNE (234CC), Fulmer Ben (700AA)—Fairholme Brew; black and blue roan.

TORMENT OF WARE (498CC), Nap—Dinah; black and white.

Photo]   FALCONER'S COWSLIP   [*Ralph Robinson, Redhill*

DOMINORUM D'ARCY (798FF), Corn Crake (692AA)—Dominorum Diana (290EE); black.

CHURCH LEIGH STORMER (1045FF), Invader of Ware, Ch. (1068DD)—Church Leigh Bess (46DD); blue roan.

GULVAL BLUE BELLE (737FF), Wolvershill Surprise—Clyst Hydon Lady; blue roan.

EXOTIC OF WARE (1047FF), Invader of Ware, Ch. (1068DD)—Exquisite of Ware, Ch. (460EE); blue roan.

OTTERSHAW RADIO (410FF), Rosemount Spot—Lady Casper; blue roan.

BLACKDOWN MIDINETTE (1816DD), Fulmer Kafir (240x) —Blackdown Soubrette (1346DD); black.

HOMESPUN OF WARE (1046FF), Invader of Ware, Ch. (1068DD)—Exquisite of Ware, Ch. (460EE); blue roan.

BRECONSIDE RUBY (1442FF), Breconside Bluestone (1033CC)—Breconside Betty; liver roan.

FELCOURT INVADER (1570FF), Invader of Ware, Ch. (1068DD)—Gnoll Floss; black and white.

BLAEDOWN BERYL (903EE), Fanfare of Ware—Blaedown Betty; black.

DELIA OF FIVE DIAMONDS, CH. (1827FF), Blaedown Bunty (502EE)—Fulmer Gleam (702AA); black.

CHAMPION MY OWN STRAIGHT SALE
American Bred

NANETTE OF WARE (262GG), Invader of Ware, Ch. (1068DD)—Church Leigh Bess (46DD); black and white.

GOODLUCK OF WARE (78GG), Invader of Ware, Ch. (1068DD)—Gnoll Floss, white and black.

FRIVOLITY OF WARE (341GG), Corn Crake (692AA)— Langmoor Vanitie (1066CC); liver roan.

GOLFHILL PRINCESS (187FF), Deemster of Ware (1667DD) —Queenie of Sauls (694EE); black.

TRUANT OF WYMING BROOK (73FF), Rocklyn Dusk (1079CC)—Rocklyn Elegance; black.

183

Rocklyn Algie (729gg), Dazzle of Dunkery, Ch. (1788dd)
—Daphne of Dunkery (812bb); blue roan.

Blackdown Daphne (830gg), Fulmer Eclipse (777dd)—
Blackdown Midinette (1816dd); black.

Wildflower of Ware (923gg), Invader of Ware, Ch.
(1068dd)—Blue Rocket; blue roan.

Dominorum Robert (1287ff), Hightown Corney (1061cc)
—Ganmor Beauty; blue roan.

Turnstone of Lydmarsh (1053gg), Invader of Ware, Ch.
(1068dd)—Moonstone (503ee); black and white.

Claremont Cobby (1181gg), Velvet Jacket—Velvet
Pansy; black.

The Dame (1186gg), Lagan Masher—Huntley Bute;
black.

Milestone of Lydmarsh (1290gg), Invader of Ware, Ch.
(1068dd)—Moonstone (503ee); blue roan.

Anthony of Ryme (1176ff), Fanfare of Ware—Moreen
of Ware; black.

Cuddlesome of Ware (1551gg), The Knut (309ee)—
The Dame (1186gg); black.

Rocklyn Critic (1641gg), Southernwood Critic (764dd)
—Rocklyn Ivy; light blue roan.

Wolvershill Meta (1830gg), Corn Crake (692aa)—
Crabble Judy; blue roan.

Dracula of Ware (419hh), Church Leigh Stormer
(1045ff)—Mayfly of Ogmore; blue roan.

Turbary Quality (664gg), Southernwood Critic (764dd)
—Falconer's Cinder (110x); blue roan.

Falconer's Daphne (1046cc), Little Dugald—Standburn
Lady (723aa); black.

Dominorum Dazzle (995hh), Invader of Ware, Ch.
(1068dd)—Church Leigh Bess (46dd); blue roan.

Beau Ideal of Ware (745hh), Coonson (663gg)—
Country Lady; black.

Gulval Bon Bon (1779gg), Vivary Crusader (409ff)—
Gulval Blue Belle (737ff); blue roan.

Wolvershill Bess (1196hh), Wolvershill Surprise—
Fairholme Truth; black and white.

Joyful Joe (261hh), Cobnar Critic—Dore Moor Jennie;
blue roan.

Pinbrook Amber (600gg), Pinbrook Colin (1593ee)—
Pinbrook Peggy (107cc); golden red.

Colinette Girlie (1325hh), Joseph—Josephine; black.

PIETHORNE MERRYTHOUGHT (1369HH), Wizard of Alkrington—Piethorne Ruby; black and white.
DOLLY TINT (768FF), Rocklyn Merryman (1080CC)—Dobrow Courtesy; blue roan.
FLAME OF SOLWAY (1148HH), The Knut (309EE)—The Dame (1186GG); black.
CHURCHDENE INVADER, CH. (1790HH), Invader of Ware, Ch. (1068DD)—Blue Rocket; blue roan.
CHURCH LEIGH BEATRIX (994HH), Church Leigh Royalist —Windus Peggy; black and white.
BELLE OF ALKINGTON (1437GG), Rocklyn Coon (1289GG) —Rowena Felbrigg; black.

Photo]   CHAMPION CHURCHDENE INVADER   [*Hedges*

SILVER WING OF AUCHINFIN (471JJ), Rocklyn Algie (729GG)—Melrose Ruth; blue roan.
IRREPRESSIBLE OF WARE (2254HH), Vivary Crusader (409FF)—Morning Light; blue roan.
BLAEDOWN BUDGET (558JJ), Blaedown Bugler (1780GG)—Sobenhal Susan; black.
FELBRIGG BRUCE (99JJ), L'ile Colonel Bogey (458HH)—Marcia of Felbrigg (828BB); black.
DOMINORUM DAPHNE (1774JJ), Dominorum Druid—Belle of Sauls (829BB); black.
CHERRYSTONE OF LYDMARSH (856JJ), Touchstone of Lydmarsh—Bluestone of Lydmarsh; blue roan.

L'ILE AUCTIONEER (920JJ), L'ile Colonel Bogey (458HH)—
Black Diadem; black.
SURF SALMO (1105JJ), Fairholme Richard—Surf Queen;
blue roan and tan.
LOVABLE OF WARE (1161JJ), Freelance of Ware (828GG)—
South Lodge Bluebell; blue roan.
HIGHBROW OF WARE (1212JJ), Corn Crake (692AA)—
Foxham Maypole (135EE); red roan.
CHARLSTON VIVANDIERE (922JJ), Vivary Crusader (409FF)
—Melrose Ruth; orange roan.
ROCKLYN VIKING (2253HH), Southernwood Critic (764DD)
—Pentir Wendy; blue roan.
FULMER PEGGY'S PRIDE (101JJ), Rocklyn Algie (729GG)—
Fulmer Margherita; blue roan.
FALCONER'S CHANCE (1582JJ), Cobnar Critic—Falconer's
Cowslip (801FF); blue roan.
DICTATOR OF WARE (330KK), Ottershaw Radio (410FF)—
Lovable of Ware (161JJ); blue roan.
ARTONE PAMELA (332KK), Joyful Joe (261HH)—Cannda-
lene Vado; blue roan.
CHURCH LEIGH STORMETTIA (449KK), Church Leigh
Stormer (1045FF)—Church Leigh Megan; blue roan.
EXPECTATION OF SOLWAY (2013FF), Broome Barney
(1450EE)—Fulmer Jill (770CC); black.
TOUCHSTONE OF LYDMARSH (579KK), Wolvershill Surprise
—Burnett Blue; blue roan.
FALCONER'S VERDICT (758JJ), Invader of Ware, Ch.
(1068DD)—Langmoor Vexation (531BB); blue roan.
RADIATOR OF SOLWAY (479KK), Rocklyn Algie (729GG)—
Church Leigh Beatrix (994HH); liver roan.
CHURCHDENE CINDERELLA (728KK), Churchdene Invader,
Ch. (1790HH)—Miss Dolly Blue; blue roan.
APEX OF WARE (580KK), Dominorum D'arcy (798FF)—
Rhapsody of Ware; blue roan.
LUCKYSTAR OF WARE (813KK), Joyful Joe (261HH)—
Wildflower of Ware (923GG); blue roan.
DOMINORUM DIAMOND (2256HH), Invader of Ware, Ch.
(1068DD)—Church Leigh Bess (46DD); blue roan.
BRIMFUL OF WARE (1127LL), Woodcock Zingari (1998EE)
—Yoredale Trix; black.
BURSLEDON DELECIA (1938LL), Dictator of Ware (330KK)
—Bursledon Dolores; black and white.

CHARLSTON LYRIC (720LL), Dominorum D'Arcy (798FF) —Charlston Idyll; black.

COBNAR FROST (1069LL), Cobnar Critic—Falconer's Cowslip (801FF); blue roan.

D'ARCYA of Oxshott (361LL), Dominorum D'Arcy (798FF)—Tynker of Oxshott; black.

FALCONER'S CAUTION (721LL), Cobnar Critic—Falconer's Cowslip (801FF), blue roan.

JOSEPHINE OF FIVE DIAMONDS (471LL), Joyful Joe (261HH)—Fulmer Dulcie; blue roan.

LINTHURST LEGEND (1071LL), Gulval Bon Bon (1779GG) —Church Leigh Rubicon (1006JJ); blue roan.

COVERTSIDE DAPHNE (1239MM), Felcourt Critic (1333JJ) —Betty of Fineshade; black and white.

DAME FORTUNE OF WARE (91MM), Dominorum D'Arcy (798FF)—Woodcock Jewel (830HH); blue roan.

FALCONER'S CLOVE (92MM), Freelance of Ware (828GG)— Falconer's Cowslip (801FF); liver, white, and tan.

GIPSYMAID OF WARE (454MM), Rocklyn Jolly Roger— Mam of Tybie; black.

VIVARY CHLOE (1812MM), Beau Ideal of Ware (745HH)— Suddon Carrie; black.

WHOOPEE OF WARE (453MM), Churchdene Invader, Ch. (1790HH)—Foxham Minx (900EE); blue roan.

BAZEL OONAH (432NN), Joker of Padson—Dunford Judy (730NN); black.

COBLEA QUEEN (1290NN), Coppington Comedian (1183LL) —Aughnaleck Judy; blue roan.

DUNFORD NIMBLE (551NN), Dominorum Donovan— Dunford Joy, Ch. (2015JJ); black.

187

The Author, MR. H. S. LLOYD with EXQUISITE MODEL OF WARE, the Cocker that many regard as the best Cocker of all times.

FALCONERS CHITA (491NN), Silver Flare of Ware (1639LL) —Falconers Caution (721LL), blue roan.

L'ILE MIDNIGHT RAIDER (967NN), Luckystar of Ware (813KK)—Melbost Maiden; blue roan.

STARDUST OF BYFLEET (1289NN), Luckystar of Ware (813KK)—Daffodil of Byfleet; red.

TREETOPS TREASURE TROVE (968NN), Bazel Otto (1154PP) —Felbrigg Hortensia (1240MM); black.

BAZEL OTTO (1154PP), Joker of Padson—Dunford Judy (730NN); black.

DOBROW DON (176PP), Churchdene Invader, Ch. (1790HH) Woodlyn Bunty; blue roan.

FALCONERS CHARITY (719PP), Foxham Midas (1760NN)— Falconers Chance (1582JJ); blue roan.

FALCONERS CONFIDENCE (720PP), Silver Flare of Ware (1639LL)—Falconers Caution (721LL); blue roan.

FELSINA OF OXSHOTT (366PP), Fullcry of Ware (173LL)— Danae of Oxshott; black.

NENE VALLEY SAINFOIN (1246PP), Woodcock Ringleader (1677MM)—Nene Valley Sunflower; red.

WANDA OF WOODHAW (886PP), Prince of Hothersall— Blue Girl of Hothersall; blue roan.

ALEXANDRAN RALLY (1142QQ), Dobrow Dash (1811MM)— Deebanks Darkie; dark blue roan.

CLEO OF BYFLEET (351QQ), Lodestar of Sorrelsun—Fay of Sorrelsun; red.

FALCONERS CAHAOUCHI (768QQ), Alexandran Crusader's Buzz (1132KK)—Falconers Clove (92MM); blue roan.

FALCONERS CAREFUL (484QQ), Silver Flare of Ware (1639LL)—Falconers Caution (721LL); blue roan.

HORSESHOE PRIMULA (590QQ), Woodcock Ringleader (1677MM)—Ottershaw Pimpernel (174LL); red.

MARKSMAN OF GLENBERVIE (1345QQ), Ottershaw Gigolo —Ottershaw Beryl; black.

MASTERMAN OF WARE (873QQ), Rydals Fearless—Storth Judy; black.

VALERIE OF MISBOURNE (688QQ), Bazel Otto (1154PP)— Vanity of Misbourne (1601PP); black.

WHIP HAND OF WARE, CH. (348QQ), Whoopee of Ware (453MM)—Bluebird of Faughan; blue roan.

WOODCOCK POLLY (1198QQ), Woodcock Ringleader (1677MM)—Woodcock Prima Donna; red.

BENET OF WARE (1257RR), Whoopee of Ware (453MM)—
Marley Betty; orange and white.

DOBROW DECORA (823RR), Dobrow Duke (718PP)—
Covertside Joy (820MM); blue roan.

FLAMENCO OF GLENBERVIE (1160RR), Ottershaw Perseus
(779PP)—Ottershaw Myrna; golden red.

FUGLEMAN OF WARE (523RR), Bazel Otto (1154PP)—
Minefreda Paulette; black.

LADY FASHION OF WARE (228RR), Whoopee of Ware
(453MM)—Foxham Leading Lady; blue roan.

MELFORT MIGNONETTE (1443RR), Dobrow Dash (1811MM)
—Fortune of the Freshwinds; blue roan.

SILVER JUBILEE OF WARE (743RR), Fortune Hunter of
Silverlands (1761NN)— Gazelle of Ware (1247PP);
blue roan and tan.

SILVER TEMPLA OF WARE (1118RR), Silver Flare of Ware
(1639LL)—Treyford Clover; blue roan.

TALLINA OF OXSHOTT (1037RR), Treetops Talkie (349QQ)
—Delvine of Oxshott (1872MM); black.

VIVARY CRACKSMAN (1922RR), Totolo Ni Theva (1879NN)
—Gulval Blue Top; light blue roan.

APPLETIME SUNSHINE SUSIE (1643SS), Appletime Sunshine
—Caleba of Alaston; blue roan.

FALCONERS CANDID (612SS), Alexandran Crusader's Buzz
(1132KK)—Falconers Careful (484QQ); blue roan.

HAPPY GIRL OF WARE (1259SS), Jeremy of Deepdene—
Pixie of Deepdene; blue roan.

PHANTASY OF SWINBROOK (243SS), Whoopee of Ware
(453MM)—Pippa of Deepdene; blue roan.

SILVER SONNET OF WARE (803SS), Silver Flare of Ware
(1639LL)—Cockerton Pamela; blue roan.

TREVILLIS ARISTOCRAT (428SS), Dobrow Dash (1811MM)
—Wribbenhall Woodsia; blue roan.

EXQUISITE MODEL OF WARE (72TT), Whoopee of Ware
(453MM)—Jane of Hubbastone; black, white, and tan.

GOLFHILL ECLIPSE, CH. (1253TT), Golfhill Pierrot (210PP)
—MELFORT MISTLETOE; black.

GULVAL SUNFLOWER (658TT), Foxham Migrant, Ch.
(2032QQ)—Gulval Bellerina (273QQ); orange and white.

RIVOLI JUBILEE QUEEN (373TT), Rivoli Desert King
(1364RR)—Copperleigh Dilys; red.

SIR GALAHAD OF WARE (70TT), Manxman of Ware (1947PP)—Falconers Confidence (720PP); black, white, and tan.
LANEHEAD ATTRACTION (1203UU), Lanehead Tradition (1197QQ)—Gratitude; black.
TREETOPS TURTLEDOVE (863UU), Treetops Terrific (71TT) Treetops Temptress (299UU); red.
WINDFALL OF WARE (862UU), Dougal of Datchet (1103SS) —Winterly of Wribbenhall; black.

Prior to June 1st, 1909, all dogs winning three challenge certificates under three different judges were entitled to the term "champion." Since that date, gun-dogs of

CHAMPION MY OWN PERFECTION
American Bred

all breeds to attain the title of champion must also obtain a working certificate in the field. Many of the dogs in the foregoing list, though winners of challenge certificates, have not qualified at field work.

An important announcement recently appeared in the *Kennel Gazette* notifying breeders that as and from January 1st, 1932, there would be an alteration regarding the registration of Spaniels, who will now be treated in exactly the same manner as Retrievers, and there will be Registers for "Inter-bred" and "Cross-bred" Spaniels. The progeny resulting from crossing, for instance, a

191

Sussex with a Cocker, will no longer be eligible for registration either as a Sussex or a Cocker, whichever it most resembles, but will only be accepted as an Inter-bred Spaniel.

Registrations made up to the end of 1931 will, of course, remain in force. This is of the utmost importance, particularly to working-bred Cockers, as many of them have from time to time been used for crossing with a Springer with excellent results. Now, until the second generation, they will have to appear in the register for "cross-breds" and will not be eligible to compete in stakes confined to a particular variety, such as a stake for "Cockers only," but it would be quite in order to enter in a stake for "Any Variety Spaniels."

Cocker Spaniels entitled to the prefix of champion since the war are as follows:—

CH. PINBROOK SCAMP (black).
CH. IRRESISTABLE OF WARE (black).
CH. L'ILE BEAU BRUMMEL (black and white).
CH. TRUCE IN OFFALY (blue roan).
CH. INVADER OF WARE (blue roan).
CH. EXQUISITE OF WARE (black, white, and tan).
CH. BLAEDOWN BUNTY (black).
CH. DOLLY TINT (blue).
CH. DELIA OF FIVE DIAMONDS (black).
CH. CHURCHDENE INVADER (blue roan).
CH. DUNFORD JOY.
CH. WHIP HAND OF WARE (blue roan).
CH. FOXHAM MIGRANT (blue roan).
CH. MARKSMAN OF GLENBERVIE (black).
CH. ALEXANDRAN JASPER (blue roan).
CH. BENET OF WARE (orange and white).
CH. HORSESHOE PRIMULA (red).
CH. STARDUST OF BYFLEET (red).
CH. VIVARY CRACKSMAN (blue roan).
CH. GOLFHILL ECLIPSE (black).

COCKERS ENTITLED TO THE PREFIX "FIELD TRIAL CHAMPION"

CH. RIVINGTON DAZZLE (black and white ticked).
CH. HEATHMYND RAMUS (liver and white).
CH. PORTSDOWN KATE (black).
CH. ELIBANK ATTENTION (black).
CH. RIVINGTON SIMON (lemon and white).
CH. SAN'S PETRONELLA (liver roan).
CH. TORNADO OF WARE (lemon roan).
CH. DALSHANGAN PETER PAN (liver roan).
CH. PAT OF CHRISHALL (liver).
CH. DANSEUSE OF FEWS (liver roan).
CH. JAZZ OF FEWS (liver roan).

F.T. CH. RIVINGTON DAZZLE

CH. AUCHENCAIRN JASPER (black and white).
CH. BARNEY OF WARE (liver).
CH. KENFIG MARY (black and white).
CH. DUSK OF FEWS (blue roan).
CH. BANCHORY RACHAEL (liver).
CH. TIPTOE OF WARE (black and white).
CH. DRUIDAIG JULIUS (black).
CH. MICHAEL OF SILVERLANDS (black).
CH. RIVINGTON PATROL (lemon and white).
CH. RIVINGTON QUICKSTEP (lemon and white).
CH. KNOB OF SILVERLAND (red).
CH. TREASURE TROVE OF WARE (black).
CH. PODDLE CRUNCH (liver and white).
CH. COLLEEN OF FEWS (red roan).

CH. RIVINGTON HOPALONG (liver and white).
CH. SUE OF SILVERLANDS (black).
CH. HEATHMYND NAP (black).
CH. AUCHENCAIRN ISA (black and white).
CH. JIG TIME OF FEWS (red roan).
CH. BARNEY'S DOUBLE OF WARE (liver).
CH. SIMON OF CORRAN (lemon and white).
CH. BEAT (black).
CH. BRAESIDE FRECKLES (black and white).
CH. DRUIDAIG PRINCE (liver).
CH. CARRAMORE AVRIL (red and white).
CH. JUDY OF BLAIR (liver).
CH. RACE-ON OF WARE (liver, roan, and tan).
CH. BROWSTER BILLOCHAN (black).
CH. GIGOLO OF FEWS (black and white).
CH. PATCH OF SILVERLANDS (blue roan).
CH. PUNCH OF BLAIR (black and white).
CH. PODDLE CRICKET (black, white ticked).
CH. PODDLE CRINKLE (black, white ticked).
CH. SMUT O'VARA (black).
CH. RAITHBURN SMUT (black).
CH. NIP OF THE LINKS (red).

MILESTONE OF LYDMARSH

APPENDIX

COMMON DISEASES OF THE COCKER SPANIEL

This Appendix is not written by the Author but is the copyright property of the publishers.

COMMON DISEASES OF THE DOG, with Special Reference to Cocker Spaniels—Their Diagnosis and Home Treatment.

BEFORE considering the actual diseases to which dogs and puppies are liable I should like to touch on a few matters of general health.

Attention to the premonitory warnings of illness is the safest way to avoid the occurrence of real disease. I have discussed exercise and diet in a previous section, but this seems a good place to deal with the subject of tone and condition in the kennel, of the troubles which do not actually amount to disease. Of these, the minor digestive disturbances are the most common. Loss of appetite is one of the most usual and should always be noticed and enquired into. After excluding mouth and teeth as the possible cause, it may be that the dog requires an alterative or stomach mixture to put him right.

In these cases we have used for the last fourteen years what we call the "Pink Medicine." I do not know the prescription, but it undoubtedly contains iron. As a tonic and restorer of appetite it is pretty well infallible; it can be had from Messrs. Stainton & Little, Veterinary Surgeons, 18, Queen's Road, Reading. The only disadvantages of the medicine are that the dogs dislike it and that it stains the teeth, but it is so efficacious that we never allow ourselves to be without it.

As a general tonic and conditioner I can recommend Karswood Powders from experience. They are specially suitable for mothers before and after whelping.

For general debility we have had the very best results with Phosferine in the liquid form.

Loss or lack of flesh generally requires some form of Cod Liver Oil. "Ostelin," which is given in single drop doses, and is also invaluable for rickets, is a very convenient means of presenting it.

For sluggish action of the bowels, which does not yield to change of diet, you may use Cascara, 2 grains sugar-coated tablets. These are specially valuable for dogs when, for any reason, they have to be shut up and deprived of exercise.

For anæmia and temporary pale noses, especially those that appear in bitches at or after coming in season, use Robin's Peptonate of Iron.

Coming now to definite illnesses, I am dividing them into sections, as under:—

A. **Diseases of Puppyhood.**

> 1, Cleft Palate. 2, Dew Claws. 3, Bad Milk in Mothers. 4, Worms. 5, Rickets. 6, Entropion. 7, Hernia.

B. **Diseases of Grown Dogs.**

> I. *Eye Troubles.*
>> 1, Injuries. 2, Ulceration. 3, Lachrymation. 4, Granular Lids.
>
> II. *Skin Troubles.*
>> 1, Insect Parasites of various kinds. Bathing. 2, Mange. 3, Riff. 4, Eczema. Sore Stops and Tails.
>
> III. *Mouth Troubles.*
>> 1, Ulceration. 2, Bad Teeth. 3, Abscesses.
>
> IV. *Contagious and infectious fevers.*
>> 1, Distemper. 2, Gastro-enteritis. 3, Influenza.
>
> V. *Respiratory Troubles.*
>> 1, Colds. 2, Bronchitis. 3, Pneumonia. 4, Chronic Catarrh.
>
> VI. *Digestive Troubles.*
>> 1, Gastritis and Foreign Bodies in Stomach. 2, Intestinal Obstruction. 3, Constipation. 4, Diarrhœa.
>
> VII. *Diseases of the mother.*
>> 1, Metritis, Acute and Chronic. 2, Breast Troubles.

VIII. *Miscellaneous*
   1, Ear Troubles. 2, Balanitis. 3, Anal Abscess.
   4, Interdigital Cysts. 5, How to Disinfect a
   Kennel.

DISEASES OF YOUNG PUPPIES
CLEFT PALATE
This malformation occurs not infrequently in new-born puppies, especially where two very short-faced strains have been mated together. The bones which form the roof of the mouth fail to join up before birth, leaving a gap leading from the mouth to the nasal cavity. The gap varies in extent, but the result is always the same. The milk comes through into the nose. These puppies cannot suck properly and never survive for long. The hind feet of cleft-palate puppies are often deformed.

DEW CLAWS
are extra rudimentary toes on the inside of the limbs; they have no function in the modern dog, and are indeed a cause of trouble, catching in the coat and leading to injury to the eyes if the dog scratches. For this reason it is always best to remove them from the back legs. The operation should be performed within a day or so of birth; use a pair of cuticle scissors, cut through the toe at the joint, close to the leg, and, if there is any bleeding, apply a little boracic powder.

BAD MILK IN THE MOTHER
is another trouble which sometimes causes the loss of puppies. They become thin and limp, or distended with wind. If not noticed in time, they very soon fade out and die one after the other. If the puppies are sucking well but do not thrive, examine the mother's milk, and if this is abundant and comes easily, it must be the quality which is deficient. Obtaining a foster-mother or hand rearing are the only courses to pursue. When puppies are left too long with the mother, especially one who has been weakened by a large litter, they sometimes develop enlargements in the neck due to disease of the thyroid gland. These " goitres " cause death, unless the puppies are quickly weaned and separated from the mother. The goitres will in time disappear if this is done; small doses of Potassium Iodide accelerate the process of disappearance.

197

WORMS

are a great nuisance in puppies, and are derived from the mother, who in her turn gets them from raw meat, or from picking up filth—a habit which is rather prevalent among all pedigree dogs. Where the mother is free from worms the puppies will not suffer from them until they begin to take raw meat. The round worm is the one most often seen in puppies. The mother's breasts should always be kept clean, especially from any contamination from the bowel. Do not treat puppies under eight weeks old for worms unless it be a matter of saving life; wait till the third month has begun in all ordinary cases. Very often the first sign of worms is their appearance in the puppy's motion; they are quite unmistakable in the case of round worms. Tape-worm looks like a tiny chain of minute flat beads. It breaks up readily into separate pieces, each of which contains eggs in immense numbers. Other signs of worms are uncertain appetite, sometimes ravenous, sometimes capricious, slime in the motions, distended stomach, dull lifeless-looking coats, and sticky eyes. Puppies with worms sometimes also develop fits caused by the internal irritation. On the whole, I think more puppies are killed by worm remedies than by worms. By no means all the advertised nostrums are effective, and all the genuine medical prescriptions require care in their administration. I am not proposing to give any prescription for the cure of worms, as I know by experience that the best results are obtained by having medicine made up fresh for each case by a veterinary surgeon who specialises in dogs. Areca nut is probably the most efficient vermifuge, but, like most potent drugs, it is also not without its risks. In adults, too, it is desirable not to let worms get the upper hand. Tape-worm should always be treated as soon as noticed, and it is a good plan to treat the whole of your kennel for worms at regular periods of about six months. Don't treat a pregnant bitch for worms; anyhow, never do so when pregnancy is advanced, or she may miscarry. A sick dog should not be dosed for worms until you are positive that nothing else is the matter; this is just where so many fatalities occur.

RICKETS

is a constitutional disease of young, growing animals, due to the absence, or deficiency, of certain elements in the diet which are necessary to healthy development. It is characterised by slight fever, softening of the bones—which may lead to malformations—and enlargement and tenderness of the joints. The puppies may be only slightly affected at first, but there is generally some lassitude and some tenderness when the affected limbs ar handled, and there is less inclination to play and take exercise. If not quickly attended to these symptoms increase, the animal " goes down on his legs," which are unable properly to support the weight of the body. The breast bone is generally flattened and the junction of the ribs with their cartilages can be felt to be enlarged, like a string of beads, along the chest on either side of the breast bone. All joints tend to be similarly enlarged. Rickets should be treated early, as the deformities which it produces are of a permanent character; the disease is, in fact, accountable for more than 80 per cent. of unsoundness in dogs. Treatment is largely a matter of diet, which should be light but very nourishing and varied. The diet should be supplemented by such preparations as Virol, which puppies take readily, administered several times a day; and, as a medicine, I have had the best results with the Emulsion of Cod Liver Oil and Hypophosphites (any reliable brand) given in doses of half to one teaspoonful three times a day, according to the size of the puppy. It is a capital medicine for the purpose, as the patients either take it satisfactorily plain or will tolerate it mixed with their diet. The treatment must be prolonged for some weeks after all symptoms have disappeared. The fact that a puppy is fat and sturdy-looking at first sight is no reason why he should not have rickets; the disease is inclined to show itself first on the biggest and bonniest of the litter. Fresh air and sunlight are essential in the kennel if rickets are to be avoided. For very young puppies which show signs of rickets the best medicine that I know is " Ostemalt," a compound of Ostelin, malt and orange juice. It is rather expensive, but very economical in use.

ENTROPION OR INGROWING EYELASHES

sometimes cause trouble. The lashes rest against the surface of the eye and irritate it; the puppy rubs with his paws, or against the furniture and turns the lashes in still further. The eyelid may be quite doubled in at the outer corner in bad cases. Naturally the irritation and rubbing before long produce ulceration of the eye. Whenever you find a " blue eye " among your puppies, with the seat of damage at the upper and outer part of the eye, look for offending lashes, especially when the trouble recurs more than once. The treatment consists in turning the lashes out and training them back whenever you have the opportunity—the more often the better; the tiniest little smear of moustache-wax will assist in holding them back. In this way slight cases can often be put right with a little patience. Extraction of the lashes is often recommended, but I have not found it very satisfactory, for it is the fine, short lashes just as often as the big coarse ones that are the worst offenders, and these are very difficult to catch hold of when it comes to extraction. Also the extracted lashes quickly grow again, and have a nasty way of beginning to turn in whilst still too short to deal with. In bad cases, then, I advise a trifling operation at the outset, which can be performed by any experienced dog surgeon. The results are nearly always permanently satisfactory. The ulceration of the eye must, of course be promptly treated.

HERNIA OR RUPTURE

in puppies is generally found in the weakly one of the litter and appears very early, often a few days from birth. It is generally first noticed after the puppy has been crying, owing to wind or other causes of stomach ache. Most ruptures are in one of two places—either at the navel or in the groin. In the latter position they may be on one side, or both. It will be recognised as a soft, slightly elastic swelling, which becomes more tense when the puppy cries, and can usually be pushed back readily, or may go back spontaneously, when the puppy is placed on its back. Many ruptures tend to cure themselves, and disappear as the puppy grows and the muscles of the abdomen acquire strength and tone. This is often the case with navel ruptures. The groin ruptures are more troublesome; though they frequently disappear in bitches, the larger ones always persist in dogs, and have been known to render them sterile, though not impotent, as stud dogs. In the case of a valuable dog I recommend an operation at an age between seven and nine months, especially where it is desired to use the dog for stud purposes. The general run of pet, or second-rate animals, should not be operated on, as the condition causes little or no inconvenience in animals which do not walk upright, and it does not, as a rule, tend to get worse, but rather to improve in adult life. I have never myself had a bitch that needed operation for hernia, though no doubt such cases do occur. When lifting a ruptured puppy, always relieve the abdominal muscles of all unnecessary strain by supporting the hindquarters. Put back the rupture as opportunity occurs, keping the puppy on its back while doing so. Ruptures are very often noticed in the weakly puppies of elderly parents, and the complaint generally has a dwarfing effect on the puppy.

DISEASES OF OLDER PUPPIES AND ADULTS

I.—Eye Troubles.

EYE INJURIES,

common in the big-eyed breeds, may range from a slight scratch—which may be quickly put right—to an accident which destroys the sight at once, and perhaps forces the eyeball from its socket. The great secret for avoiding unnecessary tragedies in this connection is to notice every injury at the very first opportunity, and to treat it before it has time to develop into a " bad eye." If your dog is blinking, ascertain the cause at once and treat it without a moment's delay. Make eye inspection and eye-washing a part of your routine, and you will save yourself endless trouble. Learn the right way to wash an eye at the start, and practise it. Even some experienced fanciers never master the art, and their dogs' eyes bear witness to the omission. You must be able to deal with all the minor cases of bad eye yourself, and be capable of applying first-aid in all serious cases while awaiting the arrival of the arrival of the veterinary surgeon.

Every beginner should have in stock and immediately available:—

> Cotton wool.
> Boracic acid in powder form.
> Soloid boric acid and zinc sulphate (Burroughs and Welcome) for making up the zinc-boric lotion (of which a small quantity may be kept ready made).

Cocaine drops for first aid, prescribed or supplied
by the veterinary surgeon.
Hot water, 100° to 105° Fahrenheit.

To wash the eye take a small glass pot, or a tea-cup
which stands steadily, and fill it with clean hot water at
100°—105° F. Tear off a few small bits of cotton wool
from the roll—pieces about the size of a haricot bean are
big enough. Drop a tiny pinch of boracic powder into the
water and let it dissolve. Stand the patient on a table and
place the left hand on the head; tilt the face up. Use the
forefinger and thumb for opening the lids, and the palm
and other fingers for firmly restraining the head from
moving. Dip one of your pieces of cotton wool into the
warm lotion and use the saturated end of the cotton wool
to guide the lotion into the eye till a considerable quantity
has spread all over the eyeball. Throw away the bit of
cotton wool, and, while still holding the head in the left
hand, bring the right hand into action to make a cup of
the eyelids, using the thumb and forefinger of both hands
to grasp the lids and gently working them in and out till
the lotion has passed into every recess. Let the lotion
escape and repeat the process several times more, using
a clean bit of wool each time. Take a dry and larger piece
of wool and dry the lids and face by gentle dabbing.
never smear or wipe the eye, except when removing hairs,
or similar soft foreign body, from the surface, and even
then wash afterward. Always clean and dry an eye before
applying a remedy to it. Whatever anyone may tell you
to the contrary, it is the best policy. Never forget to dry
the face. Repeat your treatment at intervals of an hour or
two and the cure will generally be rapid; two or three such
washings often suffice for the ordinary minor mishap, which
is so common. Where the eye is not doing so well, or
where the original injury is more severe, a bluish milky
appearance quickly extends over the surface, and the eyelids may tend to stick together in the morning, the dog
trying to keep his eye closed against the light. These are
warnings of a real bad eye, though many such yield to the
washing treatment as described, when it is properly
applied.

A really bad eye develops when the cornea gives way
and allows the inner structures of the eyeball to protrude.
This protrusion is called a " Staphyloma," and its

occurrence is always serious and must be prevented by all possible means. Once formed, Staphlyoma demands expert veterinary treatment. Do not delay a moment in obtaining advice: should the lens of the eye come out the sight of the eye will be lost and in any case disfigurement and shrinking of the eyeball are highly probable. In all the more serious eye cases, unfortunately, it is not only the primary injury that has to be dealt with, for much more serious damage is often caused by the scratching of the dog himself. This secondary injury is best provided against by making the patient wear a stiff cardboard collar, which prevents him from getting his feet near the eyes. You should keep two or three sizes of these collars in stock—one suitable for puppies, and the others for larger dogs. Where an eye is very seriously injured, or has taken a bad turn, so that you require expert advice, use the cocaine drops straight away. It is the best way of dealing with all very painful eyes. Hold the dog for some time after applying the drops, so as to give the drug time to produce its pain-relieving effects. A blow or a fight may sometimes cause the eye to be displaced from its socket, with or without injury to the eyeball. In these cases never try to push the eyeball back, but take the dog straight to the surgeon; the replacing of an eye is an operation which demands medical skill, but it is frequently completely successful where serious injury has not been inflicted on the eye itself.

ULCERATION

Ulceration of the cornea of the eye is a common complaint; it is the cause of most of the little whitish scars which sometimes disfigure the eyes. It may arise from constitutional causes, such as gastric trouble; or as a symptom of some other disease, such as distemper; or may be due to local causes, such as ingrowing eyelashes. The ulcer appears first as a slight, usual oval depression on the surface of the eye. There is surrounding inflammation, and soon the eye turns bluish or milky over the surface. The dog usually resents light, and blinks or closes the eye. Treat with the boracic lotion, as described above, for a day, then proceed to use the zinc-boric lotion, placing three or four drops in the eye after washing, and holding the dog for some minutes afterwards, as the lotion smarts a little and the dog may try to rub the eye. Zinc lotion is the best and quickest healer of a diseased eye that I know of, but it has the disadvantage of making a rather opaque white scar which is not very easy to remove completely. For this reason it does not always pay to use it where the ulcer is conspicuously (i.e., centrally) situated. In these cases Argyrol, 10 per cent., may be employed as a substitute. Colloid Argentum is another valuable preparation for early treatment of ulcers. It coats the eye with a thin film of silver chloride and is soothing and astringent in action.

GRANULAR LIDS

are due to an inflammatory condition of the "conjunctiva" —the lining of the lids—which is folded back so that it forms also the outermost covering of the eyeball. This conjunctiva (which is usually the first part to become inflamed when there is eye trouble) becomes reddened and roughened with minute soft excrescences called " granulations." These discharge a yellow muco-purulent secretion, the eye affected never looking clean or bright as it should, but spongy on the surface. The condition arises from constitutional causes which are not very clear. It becomes worse where the diet contains much biscuit, or similar starchy food. It can be inherited, certainly from the mother, possibly from the sire. The largest and most troublesome granulations are usually situated on the haw, or third eyelid—the thin glistening membrane which all dogs have in the corner of the eye. The discharge accumulates in the pouch of the lower lid, and the irritating fluid may cause frequent ulcers, which are generally the first thing to draw attention to the condition. Slight cases yield to a prolonged course of the zinc-boric lotion. Severer cases require cauterisation of the haw, which must be left to a veterinary surgeon skilled in canine eye troubles.

LACHRYMATION,

or overflowing of tears from the eye, may cause trouble by soaking the hair over the face, especially on the wrinkle, so that it falls out, or looks matted and dirty. It is due to a narrowing or closing of the little duct in the inner corner of the eye, which drains away the tears into the nose. The cause is usually a slight catarrh of the duct, which has probably extended from the nose; treatment of the nasal condition will generally put the eye trouble right.

II.—Skin Trouble.

Most of these troubles are avoidable, being due to lack of sufficient method in ensuring cleanliness, or to faulty methods of feeding. In the matter of skin troubles your aim should be prevention rather than cure.

EXTERNAL PARASITES

are accountable for the first group of troubles, and under this head I will deal with those insects visible to the eye that are sometimes found in the coat, placing the microscopic ones that live in the actual skin in a different group.

Fleas are to be found in all ill-kept dogs and occasionally get passed on to others that are properly looked after. They are merely temporarily parasitic and do not lay their eggs in the coat, but in cracks and crevices in the places where their " hosts " are likely to go. They can be a great nuisance, but are very easily got rid of.

Should you ever have to deal with a dog that is swarming with fleas, the recipe given below will end the trouble in one application:—

> Soft soap, four ounces.
> Soda, four ounces.
> Boiling water, one gallon.

Stir well in a bowl till completely dissolved, and lather the dog quickly all over, beginning at the face, and taking care to keep the rather out of the eyes. Rub the lather well into the roots of the hair all over, and after about fifteen minutes, rinse thoroughly in warm water. All places where the dog has been should be gone over with strong Pearson's, or other disinfectant, and a clean new bed made ready to receive the dog after his bath.

Ticks, where the word is properly used, are rather large blood-sucking insects whose natural host is the sheep, though they frequently get on to other animals in rural places. You generally first notice them when fully gorged with blood, as their bodies are then to be seen sticking out of the skin like small raisins, the heads and legs being firmly embedded in the skin of the dog. They generally get round the dog's neck, especially when a collar is worn. Pull them out, taking care not to break off the head, as leaving it in the skin will cause more irritation.

Lice, sometimes euphoniously described as ticks, or nits, are the most troublesome of the group. The common variety of dog-louse may be a distinct species from all others, but it generally resembles that of the wild rabbit, and I have known them to appear most mysteriously in dogs which have dealings with these animals. Luckily, dog-lice will not attack human beings, but they are not easily dislodged from a kennel if once permitted to get a firm hold. They breed very rapidly, each female laying over a hundred eggs, which hatch out in nine days. The young insects mature in another thirteen days, and lay eggs in their turn, so that it is easy to understand how quickly even a single female can cause your kennel to be overrun. In appearance the dog-louse is a very small, slow-moving, elongated greyish beast. It clings tightly to the hair, or to the skin at the roots, feeding on the particles of skin dislodged by the scratching of the dog. When numerous they may bring the dog to a low state of health through sleeplessness and scratching, so that the condition may be mistaken for mange. The true state of affairs can, however, be quickly diagnosed by the discovery of the " nits," or eggs, which are small, glistening, white objects, firmly attached to the hair, generally near the roots. Dog-lice always prefer small puppies to adult dogs, so that a bitch who has a few in her coat may be seen suckling a new-born litter simply infested with these pests. This has probably given rise to the superstition that puppies breed lice, which is, on the face of it, absurd.

The less common variety is darker in colour and is a blood-sucking parasite. It clings more closely to the skin and soon produces scabs or crusts, especially about the dog's neck. The insects are often to be found sheltering under the crusts that they have caused.

It is quite unnecessary to have lice in a kennel if sufficient vigilance be exercised. Occasional bathing with McDougall's Kür-Mange, which smells rather like cedar-wood oil and pepper, is a means of keeping all insect pests in check. Should a bad case come under your charge by purchase, or by introduction of the insects into your kennel through stud work, etc., treat by isolating the patient at once in a place which can afterwards be easily cleaned. Thoroughly disinfect or burn any bedding that the dog has

206

used, and go over the bed with a strong disinfectant. Then proceed as follows:—Bathe in strong Kür-Mange, following the directions, and leaving the coat unrinsed; repeat three days later; wait seven days so as to allow the nits time to hatch out, and repeat the two baths at three days' intervals. The dog may then be again permitted to associate with the others, which have meanwhile been thoroughly inspected in case the trouble has spread. Kür-Mange makes an excellent bath for general purposes, though perhaps a little bit drying to the skin. There is another method for getting rid of lice and their nits at a single operation; it is rather drastic, but should be employed where the case is a very bad one, the coat being already spoiled and the skin scabbed through prolonged scratching. Make a solution of *Veterinary* Izal, two tablespoonfuls to a quart of warm water, and proceed to apply it as in the direction for treating fleas. It is a very strong solution and burns the skin slightly if a delicate one; very great care must be taken not to get it into the eyes. After working the Izal in all over, removing crusts and scabs, dry off without rinsing and leave until the next day, when bathe in ordinary soap and water. The milder treatment is more suitable for ordinary cases, and must be employed where young puppies are concerned.

Whenever bathing is used as a means to destroy insects, never place the animal in the tub as for an ordinary bath, but stand him on a table, with a bowl or bath containing the washing mixture alongside, and begin at the face. When the face and head have been thoroughly dealt with down to the neck, the dog may be placed in the bath if desired. If you proceed in the ordinary way, the insects will all congregate on the head and face, the most difficult place to deal with owing to the deep stop and wrinkle and the risk of getting the stuff into the eyes. If you start with the head you drive all parasites on to the body, where they are easily dealt with.

Should a bitch in whelp (who cannot be bathed) be found to be affected with lice, smother the coat all over with boracic powder, or, better still, McDougall's "Pulvex," at intervals of two or three days, rubbing it well into the roots. This will keep the insects in check, and even sometimes gets rid of them completely before the puppies arrive.

MANGE

The next group includes the minute, practically microscopic, parasites which are responsible for mange. Mange in dogs is of two kinds, known as Demodetic (or follicular), and Sarcoptic (or common), according to the organism which causes the diease.

The first is practically incurable. It attacks young dogs under two years of age. The parasite, which is grub-like, inhabits the hair follicles and lies very deep in the skin. The whole of the coat on the chest and neck usually falls out, leaving the skin dark, wrinkled and covered with pustules. The smell is very offensive. No treatment that I know of can be guaranteed to cure Demodetic Mange; often it recurs after prolonged and seemingly successful treatment. It is best to destroy the dog. Fortunately, the disease is not very common and not nearly so infectious as common mange.

Common Mange is due to a minute spider-like insect, the Sarcoptes.

When a dog scratches furiously for no apparent reason, and continues to do so; when he rubs his face till the hair over the eyes is worn thin; when the coat has a split, broken-haired appearance, and feels harsh and unclean to the touch; when small pimples appear on the abdomen and the skin folds which connect it with the thighs; when the edges of the ears are thickened and develop enlargements like small shot; when the skin emits a strong, doggy, or almost mouse-like odour; above all, when the condition appears to be catching, so that several dogs or puppies at the same time begin to scratch, you may be perfectly sure that the trouble is *mange*.

Half the trouble caused by this complaint is due to reluctance to face facts and to call a spade a spade. If you dabble about treating it locally with ointment, not applied all over, or with a mild course of baths, or try doing a few dogs at a time, you will never be really clear of the trouble; and, though you may suppress the disease so that no dog is ever seriously affected, it will always be there, and always possess the power to infect each fresh dog that comes into your possession. You will never have first-rate coats; you will have more than your share of bad eyes; your puppies will be weakened; they will scratch and never hold their coats; and your dogs will never smell really sweet.

To cure mange completely is not difficult if you go to work in the right way and don't wait till the whole place is impregnated with the disease. Even then, if the directions here given be properly carried out, three weeks ought to see the end of the trouble; but no single precaution enumerated must be omitted. Remember that any single hair from a mangy dog may carry the parasites, and so re-infect the whole kennel, so that your procedure must be both thorough and systematic. By far the most reliable and the quickest cure in the long run is to "put the dogs in oil." Don't be persuaded to use tarry messes or disinfectant liquids of any kind, as they make the dog ill before they have killed the parasites, and do not penetrate quickly, or deeply, enough into the skin unless used dangerously strong.

Oil acts in a different way, penetrating slowly into the skin, while at the same time excluding the air and so smothering the parasites in their lairs. A well-tried old-fashioned mixture is:—

> Sweet oil,
> Black (crude) sulphur, and
> A little paraffin.

But there are several ready-made oil preparations on the market (of which I can recommend Sherley's Skin Cure from experience) which are quite satisfactory. The best way to go to work in the case of toy dogs is to select a small attic room, without carpet, which can accommodate all the patients, and where decorations and paint don't matter, and to keep the dogs in it all the time they are under treatment. Larger breeds may be housed in a *warmed* garage during the treatment, with wood-wool bedding that can afterwards be burnt. It is absolutely essential that not a square inch of the animal's body should be left unanointed, and that the oil should be rubbed into the skin and not just dabbed on the surface of the coat. Put the dog back in the isolation room after oiling and repeat the treatment three days later; then wait a week and give a third application. Three or four days later the dogs can all be bathed with soap, soda being added to the water. It generally takes

o   209

a couple of baths at least to get all the oil out, for, if the oiling has not been properly done, every hair is soaked with it. What remains of the coat after the treatment will be in a terrible tangle and should be combed out and stripped as much as possible. While the dogs have been shut away in isolation, their usual quarters are to be thoroughly purified, a regular spring cleaning and complete disinfection. Especially must every hair be removed from carpets and cushions with a damp disinfectant cloth. Sleeping places can be disinfected, washed out and re-varnished if desired, and baskets washed, dried, and, if necessary, re-varnished. All blanket bedding should be soaked in strong disinfectant for several hours before washing.

After oil treatment the new coat grows with amazing rapidity, and is often better then ever before. While the dogs are in oil, keep an extra careful look-out for bad eyes. Change the oily bedding after the first soap bath, and bring the dogs back into their usual quarters after the second. The usual slight cases that are not of long standing can be cured in eight to ten days, only two or three applications of the oil being required. The very severe cases where the skin has become thickened and wrinkled may require as long as three weeks, and as many as seven applications of oil. Kür-Mange (mentioned in the previous section) is admirable as a preventative of mange, but as a cure it acts too slowly for bad cases, or where there are a good many dogs to be treated. Unless the process be quick, there is always a risk of re-infection, and the supreme merit of the unpleasant oil treatment is that as soon as a dog is thoroughly dressed all over he at once ceases to be a source of infection to others, as all parasites anywhere near the surface are at once killed.

RIFF

is a minor skin trouble caused by a minute fungus. It takes the form of small blackish or dark brown scaly specks which adhere tightly to the dog's skin, and cause a certain amount of irritation and unsightliness. It is most generally noticed where the coat is scanty, as on the abdomen, and in the clefts between the toes. Riff is picked up in damp places, such as lawns and flower borders. Any disinfectant wash which contains sulphur and soap will remove riff in a few applications, or it may be wiped clean off with a rag steeped in a mixture of alcohol and chloroform—about two parts of alcohol to one of chloroform.

ECZEMA

is a catarrhal, inflammatory condition of the skin, causing irritation, soreness, and loss of coat, generally in patches. Any part may be affected, but it seldom extends all over the dog at the same time; the neck and chest are very often affected first. Eczema is not parasitic, but of constitutional origin, and is not infectious. It may, however, be, and not infrequently is, inherited, especially through the male line. It never spreads through a kennel; when a skin disease does that it is mange.

The disease varies considerably in form, and one variety which produces bare patches of red discharging skin is often called " Red Mange " by country practitioners. It is a misleading term, and should not be employed. Many cases closely resemble mange in appearance, but when this is the case there is no harm done if the dog be treated as mangy and put in oil. Dogs subject to eczema are inclined to have hot clammy skins and to smell stronger than they should.

Unlike mange, eczema is very difficult to treat, as hardly two cases react to treatment in the same way. It is best to let an experienced veterinary surgeon prescribe when you have tried without success for a week or two. Some cases yield to a change of diet alone, others to some particular remedy only, nothing else appearing to do the least good. Diet should be rich and nourishing, with very little in the way of biscuit or dog meal, but a good supply of raw beef. You don't see much eczema in a kennel where plenty of raw meat is used. Ointments and lotions can be applied externally to the parts affected—not all over, as in mange. A jacket may be put on to save contamination from the claws when there is much scratching. Tonic treatment such as iron and arsenic is necessary in some cases, cooling and laxative measures in others. " Sphagnol " and " Resinol " are excellent preparations for external use in the majority of cases, and Calamine Lotion is good for cooling and allaying irritation. Among dusting powders zinc oxide is much used.

Sore stops seem to belong to this group, being probably nothing but a local eczema, caused by the irritation set up through the heat and dampness in deep stops. Gently apply a little smear of boracic ointment to the tender surface for a day or so, and finish up by shaking a pinch of dry boracic or zinc oxide powder into the stop, taking care that it goes right down to the bottom. If stops are not allowed to get wet, you will see little of this complaint.

Sore tails are much less common. The complaint sometimes attacks two or three dogs at a time, generally in hot weather. The cause is a mystery to me, but from the appearance I should class it as a form of eczema. The root of the tail is affected first, though the trouble tends to spread along the shaft of the tail towards the tip, but never extends on to the body. There is a thickish yellow discharge from the skin and the hair comes off where the tail joins the body, so that the tail may be spoilt for show by the time the condition is noticed. The treatment is to wash with Condy's Fluid, strength as for external wounds, and complete the treatment as for sore stops, with boracic or zinc oxide powder. It takes about a week to ten days to cure, but the damage to the hair of the tail, if extensive, takes months to come right.

III.—Mouth Troubles.

The common troubles that need concern us are almost entirely of dental origin.

ULCERS

are often met with. In connection with all acute fevers, such as distemper, they are almost always present; in pyorrhœa, or other bad condition of the teeth, they may be very severe, attacking the edges of the tongue as well as the gums and cheeks. Such mouths can be very offensive, and may set up poisoning of the whole system. Indigestion may also produce a certain amount of ulceration, especially of the gums and cheeks. Treat the cause when found and locally use a mouth-wash of Condy's Fluid (strength as for gargle), or a saturated solution of chlorate of potash, or hydrogen peroxide ten vol. strength. Apply with a piece of cotton wool dipped in the mouthwash. Place the wool over the forefinger and gently rub it upon the gums and teeth, working it into all the recesses, and using several fresh pieces where the mouth is foul. A change of mouth-wash acts better than continuing for long periods with the same remedy.

BAD TEETH

Here prevention is the best policy. Dogs are very subject to tartar, which soon leads to pyorrhœa and loss of teeth. Bones and hard biscuit are the best removers of tartar, and regularly cleaning the teeth with a piece of fresh apple-rind is very beneficial. Where tartar has accumulated the teeth must be scaled, an operation which becomes the more painful the longer it is postponed. Some owners do their own scaling; it is not difficult, but the majority employ a veterinary surgeon. It requires care to perform, as if the gums are pushed down from the teeth in the process, pyorrhœa soon gets a hold. Where teeth are in a really bad way, they must be extracted before they cause a loss of appetite or poisoning of the system. A bad tooth left in may go on to

DENTAL ABSCESS,

an accumulation of matter about the root of the tooth, which may cause decay of the bone of the jaw in bad cases. Abscesses are most painful to the patient, and generally burst externally, either through the muzzle or under the chin, when a lower tooth is the cause. In either case permanent disfigurement of the face is likely to occur as the result of subsequent scarring. Where teeth are regularly inspected and treated, dental abscess ought never to be met with.

IV.—Contagious and Infectious Fevers.

This deadly group includes distemper in all its forms, Stüttgart disease, influenza, and infective jaundice.

DISTEMPER

Thanks to the work of the research committee organized by *The Field* Newspaper Distemper Fund, we now know something definite about the nature of this scourge. For instance, it is now established that the catarrhal, gastro-enteric and cerebro-spinal forms are all variations of the same disease, whereas Stüttgart and influenza have been shown to be quite distinct from distemper.

The only common-sense way to deal with the acute infectious diseases is by prevention, and, once the cause of distemper was finally settled, it only remained to find a really satisfactory method of preventive inoculation.

The discovery of such a method was announced about two years ago, to the great satisfaction of all the doggy community, but, on the whole, I think it may be fairly objected that that announcement was rather premature.

The method consists of a preliminary vaccination with dead material from a distemper subject, followed a week later by an injection of the actual virus of the disease. At the Mill Hill Laboratories, where the technique of the operators was faultless and the subjects were mostly hardy mongrels, the results were highly successful, but when the vaccine and virus began to be issued for general veterinary use it was not long before serious trouble appeared in certain cases. It seems that there were difficulties in standardising the strength of the virus, and my own impression is that in some cases the dose was excessive, causing after-effects such as chorea and meningitis, which were sometimes fatal. In other instances, the virus was undoubtedly dead before it came to be used, and was thus completely valueless as a preventive. Naturally there was keen disappointment among the dog public who had subscribed so generously to the research fund, specially among those whose dogs had gone through the inoculation " without turning a hair " and had afterwards developed distemper. Within twelve months the majority of the veterinary profession were afraid to recommend the Mifl Hill treatment to their clients. My personal experience was as follows: Out of a batch of seven dogs between $4\frac{1}{2}$ and 16 months old, five reacted violently to the virus and two moderately. In the course of ten days the five showed almost every possible symptom of acute distemper, but by the end of three weeks, except for loss of condition, they were through with their troubles, and I should be prepared to wager a big sum that all seven are completely immune. Recently considerable progress has been made in perfecting the treatment, in particular the virus can now be kept alive indefinitely in a dry form. It is unfortunate that the treatment should have been so discredited and the veterinary profession so alarmed by the early failures just at the time the principal difficulties were being overcome. As in all new treatments one hears a great deal of the failures and little of nothing of the successes, which I have reason to think outnumber the catastrophes by forty to one, so that after many heartburnings I can only give the advice to take the risk of inoculation rather than that of distemper. Yes, I advise you to inoculate, but the following is very important addenda:—

1. Be certain that your vet. uses the genuine Mill Hill product. If you have doubts it is as well to know that every dose that leaves the laboratory is booked in the register to the practitioner who orders it, and the register can be inspected if desired.

2. Be sure the stuff used is fresh.

3. Be sure your dog is not already sickening for distemper when inoculated. Best keep him clear of all contacts for three weeks beforehand.

4. Have the virus, or leave the whole thing alone. Two inoculations with the vaccine, as sometimes recommended, are useless; they only give a few weeks' immunity.

5. Isolate your dog after the second (virus) inoculation, and for the next fortnight treat him as if he were a distemper case *whether he reacts or not.*

6. Employ a vet. who has experience of the treatment and has mastered the technique.

If you follow this plan I don't think that you will have any reason to complain of the results, and, if your kennel is a large one, the resulting peace of mind is well worth the trouble and expense.

For those who prefer to wait and see there remain the old methods of prevention; disinfection and isolation. Common-sense precautions at shows are wonderfully effective in the case of the toy breeds and are well worth while in the larger ones. In the kennel also a little care does a long way. Isolate every dog you buy, and keep it under observation for three weeks before it joins your own. Treat every dog from another person's kennel as possibly infectious, and avoid all unnecessary contacts. Keep your dogs clear of other dogs in the street, and never permit them to sniff about in public places. Don't let strangers touch your dogs, and don't touch strange dogs yourself. When you send bitches on a visit to the stud, take them yourself and bring them back afterwards. If they *have* to spend the night in a strange kennel at such times, isolate them and keep them under observation for three weeks when they return home. If you can possibly make the accommodation, isolate your dogs after every show for the same period, so that they never come near your breeding mothers and puppies.

I do not propose to give a full account of the symptoms of the distemper group of diseases, and shall only give a few general hints as to treatment. A mere perusal of the gruesome details is enough to make a non-doggy person congratulate himself, and decide to remain dogless all his days. There are only two redeeming features about the complaint—it runs a definite course, which terminates in death or recovery in about six weeks; and it confers on the survivors a considerable degree of immunity from future attack. The mortality rate is very variable and depends principally on three factors:—

1. Early diagnosis.
2. Good nursing.
3. Separation of the cases.

1. Get accustomed to using a clinical thermometer in your kennel; a feverish dog has not *always* got a hot nose. The temperature of a dog is taken in the rectum, the thermometer being well vaselined before introducing it. It is the only reliable test of fever. If you really look at your dogs and study their ways, you will detect trouble almost before it arrives. You will tell at once when they are out of sorts. Where one dog is feverish and out of sorts, isolate and watch it. It may be the one that is starting the trouble, and, if isolated in time, the others may yet escape. If several dogs develop temperatures at once, be very suspicious, and treat them as if they were actual distemper cases. Where vomiting and diarrhœa, or colds in the head and inflamed eyes appear in several dogs at once, suspect distemper at once and act quickly. The different forms of the disease vary so greatly that the symptoms as a whole are never the same in two successive outbreaks. The one symptom always present is fever. Normal temperature in a dog is $100\frac{1}{2}°$ Fahrenheit; in puppies up to a degree more. Any temperature above this point constitutes fever. Another early symptom in all forms is discoloration of the teeth, which are coated with a blackish fur, not tartar, which is exactly like the effect produced by a course of iron medicine on human teeth. The breath is always foul and the gums tender and ulcerated. In the typical, catarrhal form of the disease, nasal discharge is an early symptom and may be very

216

prominent, and there may be a reddish spotty rash on the abdomen at a very early stage, even before the first signs of illness are apparent; but this is not an invariable symptom. Inflammation of the eyes occurs early in the typical form. Another common form of the disease is gastro-enteritis, or " septic catarrh of the bowels," in which the onset is far more gradual and indefinite. It is quite possible to be suffering from this complaint in your kennel for days before it is definitely recognised for what it is. Vomiting is usually present, diarrhœa always. The motions are dark but not absolutely liquid, and contain mucus and generally blood; there are remarkable intermissions and relapses, each relapse being accompanied by a big rise of temperature. It is in this form that the highest distemper temperatures are noticed. I have had recoveries in dogs which have shown 108°—109° F. for several days in succession. Neither nasal discharge nor cough are noticeable features, and the eye symptoms appear rather later than in ordinary distemper, and may be very severe in some outbreaks, practically absent in others. Gastro-enteritis is not nearly so deadly to puppies; in our experience we have never lost a puppy from the disease. On the other hand, it is absolutely fatal to bitches in whelp, who invariably miscarry, and may die in a few hours from contracting the complaint. Not one in four makes a recovery, as metritis always follows the miscarriage. With ordinary distemper the mother may usually be saved, but the puppies are always lost; puppies, on the whole, stand much less chance than adults with the ordinary form of the disease.

Most of the preparations marketed as cures for distemper are internal disinfectants, and, as such, might assist the dog in resisting the disease. Apart from this, the treatment consists of nursing, i.e., watching the symptoms and trying to relieve them as they appear.

Mouths should be washed out and eyes bathed at frequent intervals. No solid food should be given till temperatures have been reduced to normal and remain so for some ten days. The invalid diet may consist of Benger's Food, or other similar preparations, condensed milk made up with barley water, milk beaten up with white of egg, raw beef juice freshly prepared, Brand's Essence and similar preparations, while the temperature remains high and the symptoms severe. As the condition improves, milk puddings, such as arrowroot, cornflour and custard, and small quantities of finely-divided boiled fish can be introduced, but you must wait until the dogs have been showing a normal temperature for ten consecutive days before giving raw meat and such-like heavy foods. Brandy, in water, should be used for collapse and heart weakness. Raw white of egg may be shaken up with the drinking water where vomiting and diarrhœa are troublesome. High fever may be reduced by the use of one of the internal disinfectants such as glycerine and carbolic, or by small pills of aspirin and quinine, or by homœopathic aconite, which is very successful with small dogs. I have tried aspirin in tabloid form, but find that it is nearly always vomited. Nasal discharge, cough and lung symptoms are relieved by impregnating the atmosphere of the room with Vapo-Cresolene, or similar compound. Threatened pneumonia may be dealt with by the steam kettle, in which a couple of teaspoonfuls of Friar's Balsam have been placed.

Brain symptoms such as fits should be treated with bromide of potassium and the application of an ice-bag to the head.

Each dog attacked by distemper must have his own quarters where no other can get near him. This is of great importance, and has much influence in lessening the severity of the attack. A little sweetened condensed milk added to the drinking water will often sustain strength when no other food is being accepted; in these circumstances also the raw beef juice, given two teaspoonfuls at a time every hour or so, is a very valuable measure, but must not be used when brain symptoms threaten. A flannel jacket round the body, with holes placed well apart for the forelegs, and sewn up along the back so that it reaches to the loins, is generally advisable in all cases. It saves lung trouble as a rule, and in wintry weather it is indispensable. The sick-room should be kept at an even temperature between 60° and 70° Fahr.; ventilation is most necessary, but the patients must on no account be exposed to draughts. Never be tempted to give a solid meal to a patient because he is asking for it; if the temperature is not steadily down it will only cause a relapse.

Influenza has the appearance of a mild form of the ordinary catarrhal distemper, so far as symptoms are concerned, but there are intermediate cases which appear to partake of the nature of both. Fever, some sort of nasal discharge, and some amount of eye trouble, are always present, and cough may be noticed in the later stages. With ordinary nursing precautions there are no relapses, the complaint running its course in about fourteen days and recovery being complete by the fourth week. Treat as for distemper.

Stüttgart disease, or canine typhoid, is distinct from distemper; neither disease confers immunity from the other. It occurs in local epidemics at irregular intervals and has sometimes occurred after dog shows, though, fortunately, it appears to be much less " catching " than distemper. The symptoms are those of a violent gastro-enteritis. There is constant vomiting, which very soon becomes fœtid and blood-stained. Extreme ulceration of the mouth is an early symptom, the mucous membrane of the tongue and cheeks becoming gangrenous and sloughing off. The mortality must be well over 80 per cent. for all cases and is nearer to 100 per cent. in pedigree dogs. Prompt isolation of cases will prevent the disease spreading as I have twice proved from personal experience. Death may take place within twenty-four hours of the first signs of illness, other cases survive for several days. Treatment should be directed to constant cleansing of the mouth; apart from that, large hypodermic injections of hot normal saline solution offer the best chance of recovery. Other treatment as for distemper.

Infective jaundice. The cause of this disease has only been recently recognised. The source of infection is the rat, who communicates the infection to the dog's food or to his living-quarters. The symptoms resemble the gastro-enteric form of distemper with the addition of a slight but perceptible jaundice. Prevention of the disease by avoiding contamination by rats is, of course, the best course, but, should a case occur, there is an effective inoculation which cures if administered in time. Other treatment as in distemper.

COLDS

Slight colds occur owing to wettings, or in cold windy weather, and generally show themselves by an unusual amount of sneezing or snuffling; when neglected they may go on to something worse, so it is always as well to keep a dog with a cold indoors in a warm place. See that he does not get wet, and clear the nose by putting a drop of eucalyptus on his chest so that he is obliged to inhale it. If you put it on the nose he licks it off at once, so it does very little good and gives dire offence to the dog. You will save many colds if in wet weather you will rub over the feet and under-parts with a rough towel after exercise.

BRONCHITIS

may attack dogs or puppies that have caught cold, and may be recognised by the difficulty of breathing which at once appears. Place your ear to the chest and listen; bubbling noises are heard and the sound of the breath is whistling as if air were passing through a pipe. The patient may open his mouth in order to breathe better and may refuse to lie down. Put on a jacket at once and keep the dog in an even temperature, steam with Friar's Balsam, or use the Vapo-Cresolene outfit. When taken promptly these cases generally do well; if neglected they may turn to

BRONCHO PNEUMONIA

This is always a most serious complaint. It is characterised by rapid difficult breathing, cough, and fever which may be very high. It may occur as a complication of other diseases, such as distemper, or may follow a chill or a neglected cold. Cough is always a serious symptom in a dog, indicating some degree of lung trouble; treat generally as for bronchitis; an Anti-phlogistine jacket is sometimes useful, though it means messing up the coat badly. The strength must be husbanded and the heart's action carefully watched, stimulants being administered as required. The attendance of a veterinary surgeon is most desirable, unless the dog owner be well experienced in nursing.

CHRONIC CATARRH

All the short-nosed breeds are rather subject to this complaint. It is generally one of the troubles of elderly dogs and causes a certain amount of discomfort through nasal obstruction and difficulty in breathing when the mouth is closed. Dogs with contracted nostrils are specially subject to it. After a sneezing attack a certain amount of thick mucus may be noticed at the nostrils, and it is the accumulation of this in the passages which obstructs the breathing. The condition is improved by warm weather and accentuated by cold winds. There is no satisfactory permanent cure, but the condition may be relieved with eucalyptus, used as for colds, and by injecting " Inhalone," or similar compounds, into the nostrils. I do not believe that this condition greatly affects the health, or materially shortens life.

VI.—Digestive Troubles.

GASTRITIS

This is an inflammation of the lining of the stomach and is due to irritation set up by poisonous or indigestible substances; or it may be a symptom in the course of some other acute disease, such as distemper, and especially gastro-enteritis. When acute and severe, the onset is generally very sudden. The animals vomits, and after emptying the stomach, continues to retch, and from time to time brings up frothy mucus which may be stained with blood. Collapse is very rapid, the animal becoming prostrated. He generally lies in a dark corner, or hangs his head over a bowl of water, but does not drink. In other cases they may drink large quantities and vomit it up again. Gastritis is a serious condition, as poisoning is at once suggested. If you suspect that the dog has swallowed something hard and indigestible, such as a sharp stone, give liquid petroleum, one dessert-spoonful, with which about five grains of Bismuth Sub-Nitrate may be mixed, and continue this treatment at intervals of four hours, applying hot compresses to the belly to relieve pain. If, on the other hand, the dog has taken something poisonous and has vomited all he is able, your treatment should be to clear the poison from the system by means of castor oil administered as quickly as possible. It is a curious thing

221

that castor oil, even though the greater part of it may be vomited, always seems to act to some extent and to produce a movement of the bowel more quickly than any other drug. A possible sharp foreign body may be suspected when vomiting is not such a prominent feature, but the dog shows obvious signs of stomach ache, groaning when he is picked up in the usual way. Here your aim is to float the object away without damaging the stomach and intestine; that is why the liquid petroleum should be used. Petroleum is not an aperient, but a lubricant. In all gastric cases the first-aid measures should be followed up by several doses of Bismuth Sub-Nitrate, or Bismuth Carbonate. This drug coats the lining of the stomach, thus protecting it from irritation. No solid food should be given for a day or two at least.

INTESTINAL OBSTRUCTION,

when complete, at once causes grave symptoms of illness. Violent straining and retching generally occur and collapse rapidly follows. Operation is the only possible chance, but you will generally be too late. Hair and pieces of woollen fabric swallowed by dogs not infrequently cause partial or temporary obstruction, indicated by distention of the stomach, vomiting and straining without results. Treat with internal (liquid petroleum), and give an injection of soap and water per rectum. This will generally move the obstruction. Castor oil is not suitable where there is anything which can clog into a mass, or damage the bowel.

CONSTIPATION

is best treated by dieting measures, as all drugs taken as purgative tend to have a reaction in the opposite direction. This does not apply to a mere lubricant such as petroleum, which can always be safely given. Most of the biscuit meals and other patent foods tend to relax the bowels, as also does horse-meat. Milk is rather constipating food. Brown-bread crumbs, moistened with good rich gravy, are excellent for keeping the bowels regular in young puppies. Of drugs, cascara can always be given safely. It is only a laxative where dogs are concerned and may be administered for several days in succession if necessary.

Chronic metritis is a disease of elderly bitches, caused by degenerate changes in the womb and ovaries. It is characterised by a thick purulent discharge which soon becomes continuous. The condition is associated with slight intermittent fever. The only treatment that avails is immediate operation, douching is quite useless, as the mouth of the womb remains closed. The operation, if undertaken before general blood poisoning has set in, is generally completely successful, life being prolonged for years, and perfect health quickly restored. A bitch that has been so operated upon is not allowed by Kennel Club rule to compete in a show.

BREAST TROUBLES

is nursing mothers sometimes cause anxiety. One cause of worry may be an excessive flow of milk which cannot be sufficiently relieved by a small litter. The breasts " knot," becoming hard, tender and hot, and the puppies will not take to them. The treatment consists of applying hot towels to the breast, and then very gently drawing away the milk with the finger and thumb till the tension is eased, after which the puppies must be persuaded to take the affected breast.

Sometimes the nipple of one or more breasts is blind, so that milk accumulates in the gland but cannot escape; the treatment is to carefully draw off the milk from the breast or breasts nearest to the blind one, and to see that the puppies take these regularly. The blind breast will then generally go down. To get rid of milk after the puppies have died, or been transferred to a foster-mother, gently massage the breast with a half-and-half mixture of methylated spirits and water. Small doses of antropine internally will hasten the result.

VIII.—Miscellaneous Troubles

EAR TROUBLE OR CANKER

may be very troublesome to the dog, causing him to scratch and tear at his ear, not infrequently giving himself a bad eye in the process. Sometimes the ears are visibly inflamed about the passage to the drum, and wax and dirt accumulate in it; at other times there are no external signs, the ear appearing perfectly clean, but the irritation is there just the same. It is only quite recently that I have

Chronic metritis is a disease of elderly bitches, caused by degenerate changes in the womb and ovaries. It is characterised by a thick purulent discharge which soon becomes continuous. The condition is associated with slight intermittent fever. The only treatment that avails is immediate operation, douching is quite useless, as the mouth of the womb remains closed. The operation, if undertaken before general blood poisoning has set in, is generally completely successful, life being prolonged for years, and perfect health quickly restored. A bitch that has been so operated upon is not allowed by Kennel Club rule to compete in a show.

BREAST TROUBLES

is nursing mothers sometimes cause anxiety. One cause of worry may be an excessive flow of milk which cannot be sufficiently relieved by a small litter. The breasts " knot," becoming hard, tender and hot, and the puppies will not take to them. The treatment consists of applying hot towels to the breast, and then very gently drawing away the milk with the finger and thumb till the tension is eased, after which the puppies must be persuaded to take the affected breast.

Sometimes the nipple of one or more breasts is blind, so that milk accumulates in the gland but cannot escape; the treatment is to carefully draw off the milk from the breast or breasts nearest to the blind one, and to see that the puppies take these regularly. The blind breast will then generally go down. To get rid of milk after the puppies have died, or been transferred to a foster-mother, gently massage the breast with a half-and-half mixture of methylated spirits and water. Small doses of antropine internally will hasten the result.

VIII.—Miscellaneous Troubles

EAR TROUBLE OR CANKER

may be very troublesome to the dog, causing him to scratch and tear at his ear, not infrequently giving himself a bad eye in the process. Sometimes the ears are visibly inflamed about the passage to the drum, and wax and dirt accumulate in it; at other times there are no external signs, the ear appearing perfectly clean, but the irritation is there just the same. It is only quite recently that I have discovered a completely satisfactory treatment in the latter group of cases. It is in powder form, and is prepared by Mr. Male, Veterinary Surgeon, of Friar Street, Reading. A little pinch dropped well into the cavity of the ear soon brings up a quantity of irritating material, whose presence could never have been suspected from ordinary examination, and the condition of the ear quickly becomes normal. The powder is yellowish white and smells of iodoform; I do not know its exact composition, but can strongly recommend it. Neglected cases may turn to abscess in the ear, which is very painful and not very easy to treat. The best preventive of canker is to keep the ears clean, and never allow water to get into them when bathing. Before a bath always plug the ears with pieces of dry cotton wool, but don't forget to remove them afterwards.

BALANITIS

This complaint is very common in male dogs, and is characterised by a yellow discharge from the sheath of the penis. The sheath must be well syringed out from time to time with a small glass syringe, using a solution of zinc sulphate, three grains to one ounce of water. Hold the solution in the sheath for a minute before allowing it to escape.

ANAL ABSCESS

These painful swellings occur through the blocking of the ducts of one or other of a pair of small glands that lie on either side of the anus. The dog affected keeps his tail down and screams when passing his motions. A dog who suffers in this way is generally in a run-down condition and inclined to constipation. I do not think that lancing of the abscess is necessary, as it can be rapidly ripened by gently sponging with hot water, when it soon breaks through the skin and the matter escapes. Wash out the cavity of the wound by syringing with Condy's Fluid, but don't encourage it to close up too quickly; it should be allowed to heal up from below, the opening being kept clear as long as possible to permit all discharge to escape.

INTERDIGITAL CYSTS

are blister-like swellings which appear between the toes, causing irritation and discomfort. A dog so affected is always liable to develop them again and again. They are probably of bacterial origin, but are not catching. Treatment is not at all satisfactory, but some cases are certainly cured by inoculations. The cysts should be pricked, squeezed and swabbed out with Tincture of Iodine.

DISINFECTION AFTER ILLNESSES

After any infectious illness, systematic disinfection of your kennel should never be neglected, and must be carried out before you attempt to exhibit again at shows or receive any new stock into your kennel. In discussing mange I have given directions for dealing with infected accessories, such as boxes, beds, basket and bedding, but every article used for the dog, not forgetting combs and brushes, must be similarly dealt with if safety is to be assured. Fresh air and bright sunlight, when available, are great germicides, so all operations upon kennel accessories are best conducted in the open air, and the cleansed articles should be left to stand some time in sunlight and air. The sick-room, after being stripped of all hangings, curtains and loose articles (which must be separately disinfected according to their nature) should be scrubbed out with a good disinfectant such as Pearson's. All air openings should then be blocked up, and Formaline candles to a number dependent on the size of the room (see directions) should be lighted. Hurry out of the room, carefully closing the door behind you, and come up in two hours' time to open the windows and get rid of the irritating fumes of the Formaline. Sulphur candles are of very little use. Formaline, in one or other of its preparations, is essential for thorough disinfection.

Lightning Source UK Ltd.
Milton Keynes UK
04 January 2011

165157UK00001B/215/A